Advance Praise for
The Journey Through Grief and Loss

"*The Journey Through Grief and Loss* is a great gift for parents or other adults trying to assist their child or children even as the adult copes with loss. It offers great sensitivity, cutting-edge information, and sage advice for those who must take care of themselves even as they reach out to others."

> —Kenneth J. Doka, Ph.D., professor of gerontology, College of New Rochelle, and senior consultant to the Hospice Foundation of America

"For too long you, the parent of a grieving child, have been left behind to struggle with your own grief and loss. Finally, Robert Zucker's outstanding new book will provide you with the information and inspiration you'll need to take your child by the hand and walk together on your difficult yet hopeful journey."

> —Joy Johnson, cofounder of the Centering Corporation, coauthor of *Tell Me, Papa*, and *Children Grieve, Too*

"In the midst of their own sorrow and pain, grieving parents are often at a loss for how to help their children. This book provides practical information in an easy-to-read format to help grieving parents better understand and support their bereaved children. I highly recommend this book!"

> —Liana Lowenstein, M.S.W., author of
> *Creative Interventions for Bereaved Children*

"Powerful! A must-read that contains insightful grief wisdom with practical, hands-on suggestions that offer both hope and healing for the adult and child through the perilous journey of loss."

—Earl A. Grollman, D.H.L., D.D., inspirational speaker and author of *Living When a Loved One Has Died*

"*The Journey Through Grief and Loss* is thoughtful, practical, and caring. Robert Zucker understands the challenges of parents juggling both their own grief and the needs of their children. His words are shared with warmth and compassion, coupled with the wisdom he has gained in decades of listening to adults and children pour out their loss."

—Donna Schuurman, Ed.D., F.T., executive director of the Dougy Center for Grieving Children & Families and author of *Never the Same*

THE

❧ JOURNEY ❧

THROUGH GRIEF

AND LOSS

THE JOURNEY THROUGH GRIEF AND LOSS

Helping Yourself and Your Child When Grief Is Shared

ROBERT ZUCKER, M.A., L.C.S.W.

ST. MARTIN'S GRIFFIN

New York

THE JOURNEY THROUGH GRIEF AND LOSS. Copyright © 2009 by Robert Zucker. All rights reserved. Printed in the United States of America. For information, address St. Martin's Press, 175 Fifth Avenue, New York, N.Y. 10010.

www.stmartins.com

Design by Kathryn Parise

Grateful acknowledgment is given for permission to reprint the following:

"Birdsong," edited by Hana Volavkova, from *I Never Saw Another Butterfly* by U.S. Holocaust Memorial Museum, edited by Hana Volavkova, copyright © 1978, 1993, by Arita, Prague Compilation © 1993 by Schocken Books. Used by permission of Schocken Books, a division of Random House, Inc.

Some of the materials by Robert Zucker that are included in this book were first published in the CareNotes series by Abbey Press and are reprinted here by permission of Abbey Press.

LIBRARY OF CONGRESS CATALOGING-IN-PUBLICATION DATA

Zucker, Robert.
    The journey through grief and loss: helping yourself and your child when grief is shared / Robert Zucker. — 1st ed.
        p. cm.
    Includes bibliographical references.
    ISBN-13: 978-0-312-37414-3
    ISBN-10: 0-312-37414-3
    1. Grief.   2. Grief in children.   3. Grief therapy.   I. Title
    BF575.G7Z83 2009
    155.9'37—dc22   2009010882

First Edition: August 2009

10 9 8 7 6 5 4 3 2 1

∾ DEDICATION ∾

Between 1941 and 1945, approximately 139,000 European Jews were rounded up, loaded into cattle cars, and taken to Terezin Concentration Camp, outside Prague. Among them were parents, teachers, clergy, social workers, musicians, writers, composers, and visual artists who worked together, at great personal risk, to create a secretive, safe haven for thousands of boys and girls also imprisoned. As a result of their efforts, with death all around them, the children of Terezin wrote poems, drew and painted, played their musical instruments, published an underground newspaper, and sang out their stories. Nearly all of the Jews at the camp were brutally murdered, and only one hundred out of approximately fifteen thousand children imprisoned at Terezin survived the war. But some of their voices have survived and can still be heard today, because the adults at Terezin gave their children hope.

This book is dedicated to the men and women throughout history who were willing to embrace their children as they suffered together, and to the memory of one child, whose name will forever be unknown, who left us a poem from those days in Terezin, which is the epigraph for this book.

∞ CONTENTS ∞

❧ ACKNOWLEDGMENTS ❧

My heartfelt thanks to Rabbi Earl Grollman, Sandra Bertman, Phyllis Silverman, Linda Goldman, Donna Schuurman, Ken Moses, and the late Sandra Fox, for shaping my understanding of grief; Eva Gumprecht and Nick Belsky, for their wisdom, passion, and mentorship at Antioch; Dan Grippo at Abbey Press; Barry Sachs, M.D.; and Agnes Mauro and Joy and Marv Johnson, for writing great books like *Tell Me, Papa,* and for supporting fledgling writers; Helen Fitzgerald, for her kind support; Donna O'Toole, for her generous heart, brilliant work, and wise counsel; Bruce Greene, for his friendly guidance at Compassion Books; Sister Mary McCue, for her loving, compassionate, humble spirit; Jack Jordan, for his wisdom, humor, friendship, and for being a great teaching partner for many years; David Browning, for his kind, collegial spirit and friendship; Kathy Brunner and Judith Skretny at CMI; Jonathan Diamond, for knowing I had a book to write, showing me how to begin, and introducing me to my excellent literary agent, Susan Lee Cohen; P. J. Dempsey, for editorial support; Maureen Buchanan Jones, who knew just how to help shape my book with kind, incisive comments, questions, and invaluable editorial assistance; my wife, Andrea Zucker, for her constant love and support, patience, and wise, thoughtful editing; Sophia Zucker and her partner, Laura Hilberg, for their insightful and loving assistance in Glover, Vermont, where this project took flight; Zachary Zucker, for his wisdom and beautiful music; Alyse S. Diamond at St. Martin's Press, for her excellent editorial guidance; all of the nurses and doctors I've worked with over the years, for their courage, hard work, dedication, and inspiration; the tens of thousands of helping professionals who attend my seminars and listen to my stories; the hundreds of children, adults, and families I've worked with over the years who have opened their hearts to me during the toughest times in their lives and taught me more than I ever imagined possible. To my first family, Diane, Cliff, Mark, and Mom and Dad.

Birdsong

He doesn't know the world at all
Who stays in his nest and doesn't go out.
He doesn't know what birds know best
Nor what I want to sing about,
That the world is full of loveliness.

When dewdrops sparkle in the grass
And earth's aflood with morning light,
A blackbird sings upon a bush
To greet the dawning after night.
Then I know how fine it is to live.

Hey, try to open up your heart
To beauty; go to the woods someday
And weave a wreath of memory there.
Then if the tears obscure your way
You'll know how wonderful it is
To be alive.

—Anonymous, 1941

THE
✼ JOURNEY ✼
THROUGH GRIEF
AND LOSS

∞ INTRODUCTION ∞

It is a beautiful autumn day in the Connecticut countryside, where I am leading a weekend retreat for bereaved parents and siblings. At morning meeting, all of the children at the retreat, ranging in age from five to eighteen, are encouraged to think about any concerns they've had since the death of their brother or sister, and, at some point during the day, to go to the lobby of the retreat center where they will find a cardboard box sitting on a side table, alongside a stack of paper and some pencils. This is their Concerns Box, and they are told to write down any worries they have on a piece of paper and place them anonymously inside the box. No names are required in hopes that the children will feel free to write about anything that is worrying them. Later, after dinner, about twenty children sit in a circle as I draw from the Concerns Box. One by one I read aloud what they have written, and attempt to address each child's concern. Three themes emerge. First, several of the children blame themselves for the death of their brother or sister. One six-year-old has written, "I think I made my sister die." Second, many of the children feel abandoned by their parents, and even, in some cases, that they are in competition with their dead sibling. A nine-year-old girl asks, "Why does my mommy wish that I died instead of my brother?" And finally, there are a number of children in the circle who are concerned that their parents are not coping well. One teenager writes, "I worry about my father not getting through this."

As I listen to the concerns of these young people, it strikes me how grieving adults can become so overwhelmed that they lose sight of their obligations to their grieving children. The idea for this book was born three years ago out of that retreat as I realized that there needed to be a single book for grieving adults who required support and concrete advice for themselves, but who also desired to learn how they could help their grieving children.

I've written *The Journey Through Grief and Loss* because parents like you need to get beyond hopelessness and despair and find new hope for you and your child. If, like many adults, you grew up in a family that never discussed death and grief and assumed children didn't grieve at all, or if your child's expression of grief has been heightening your own pain and you can't bear your child's sorrow any longer, then this book is for you. If you've tried blocking out your own grief in order to be available to your child, and yet your child can still see how much you're suffering, then this book is for you. If you can barely manage to keep your own head above water, and sometimes you resent your children for demanding more of you now than ever before, or if you are so bereft that you sometimes forget about everyone else around you, including the children in your life, then this book is for you.

Families have much to gain once adults master the skills to manage their own grief and to support their grieving children. Children discover that they can count on loving adults to guide them through even the toughest times imaginable. Parents and children understand and appreciate one another more than ever before. And eventually, families can discover new strengths, and hope can be restored. Nothing can take away the pain of grief, but I hope you can use this book like a wise and caring friend, to help you gain the wisdom and strength to meet the challenges ahead.

This book is divided into five parts. Part One is an overview of the road ahead of you. In addition to considering some of the basic differences between adult and childhood grief, I will break grief into three phases: Embarking on the Journey (early grief), The Second Storm, and The Search for Meaning.

During early grief you're lost and overwhelmed. It is a time when you can't fully believe what is happening, and you struggle with periods of anxiety and, perhaps, numbness. In the Second Storm you may face feelings so intense that it will seem as if you're going crazy. You'll enter the Search for Meaning once the storm has settled a bit and you're better able to consider life's bigger questions and how your loss has affected your feelings about the future.

Part Two explores early grief in greater depth. You will gain a better understanding of how grief is affecting you and your child, ways of taking care of yourself, strategies for helping your child understand what has actually happened, and techniques for helping your child start to grieve well. Included in this section are suggestions for determining whether or not your child should attend a funeral, as well as strategies for you and your child to return to work and school as smoothly as possible.

In Part Two, as in all subsequent sections of the book, when strategies for understanding and assisting young people are discussed, they are addressed according to age groups: preverbal, two- to five-year-olds, six- to nine-year-olds, ten- to twelve-year-olds, and adolescents.

Part Three explores the second phase of grief, which I call the Second Storm. As the name suggests, this phase of grief will shake you up like a tornado, but you'll learn to find your own footing so that you can help your child express and share the overwhelming feelings that are likely to surface. This section also debunks two common myths about grief: that everyone grieves in a similar way, and that grievers feel helpless all the time. In fact, there are actually ways you can learn to grieve well together. Part Three will help you identify and understand your own way of grieving, as well as your child's. This section will also explain what to do if your style of parenting doesn't quite meet your child's needs at this difficult time.

Part Four will explore the third phase of grief, the Search for Meaning. You'll learn how you and your child can come out of the storm prepared to consider what your loss has meant for you and your family, what you each have learned, and how you and your child have been changed as a result of your circumstances. This section looks at ways to keep memories alive through a range of informal activities for you and your child that will encourage reminiscence. This section also looks at ways you and your child may begin to feel the presence of your loved one over time.

Part Five will help you determine when it is advisable to seek additional support beyond the scope of this book, for you and/or your child, and how to identify the resources you'll need in your community. There is also a list of grief support centers, organized by state.

The annotated bibliography in the back of the book will provide further help to you and your child as you grieve together.

You and your child have begun a journey you never asked to take. It will be difficult and sometimes frightening, but if you walk together, hand in hand, I believe you will find solace, hope, new joys, and, perhaps, reasons to celebrate again. I invite you to take this book with you as you embark on the difficult road ahead.

PART ONE

PREPARING FOR THE JOURNEY

∽ | ∽

Death Changes Everything

The world as you once knew it is shattered by a death that has left a profound void in your life. Whether this death was sudden or you had time to prepare, you are probably feeling disoriented and in deep shock. As a parent, however, there is a particular gravitas to your grief: A child you love is sharing your loss. Even as this most profound of losses is shaking you to the core, you must somehow rise to the challenge and assist your child, who is also grieving.

Like adults, children grieve when someone close to them dies. Whether your child has lost a parent or a sibling, a grandparent or a dear friend, you need to be there to provide support, guidance, reassurance, honesty, and patience. Most important, you need to provide a strong and loving presence.

There Are Many Faces of Grief

The first step of your journey through grief is to appreciate that you and your child may grieve differently. There are as many ways to grieve as there are grievers, so don't try to fit your grief into anyone else's mold or expectations. While some grievers cry day and night, others feel completely numb. While some are exhausted and feel the need to nap frequently, others may stay awake for days. Some may be ravenously hungry while others have no appetite at all. Some need to talk while others long for solitude, and some experience heightened libido while others lose all interest in sex. In later chapters we'll look closely at various styles of adult grief, for now it's simply important to remember that for both children and adults, normal grief has many faces.

How Children Perceive Death

Children grieve differently from adults. Up to the age of ten, they will typically have difficulty understanding what death means. There are three reasons why this is so:

1. Young children often aren't given accurate, age-appropriate information about what death means.
2. It takes them a long time to fully appreciate the meaning of death itself, since they have trouble grasping some basic concepts about death.
3. Young children are likely to blame themselves unnecessarily whenever someone they love dies. This is called "magical thinking."

Children of all ages tend to believe they have somehow caused the death, and correcting this view is different for younger ones than it is for preteens and teens.

Later in this book we'll go over how to explain the facts of a death clearly and accurately to a child of any age. For now, we'll simply focus on what helps kids of various ages understand the concept of death. In a quick summary:

- Preverbal children often need comfort more than words.
- Two- to five-year-olds typically struggle with the fundamental concepts that determine a death and require loads of patience.
- Six- to nine-year-olds tend to become overwhelmed by the notion that death is universal, benefiting from appropriate information and a great deal of reassurance.
- Preteens grasp the concept of death but tend to intellectualize their loss. They need to be listened to and respected.
- Teens often bring a tricky emotional package to their grief and require careful attention and support.

The Three Phases of Grief

There are three rather predictable phases on the grief journey for adults and children alike:

Phase One: Early Grief: During early grief you may struggle to come to terms with the reality of what has happened. Consequently, your earliest reactions might be a defiant denial, high anxiety, or numbness.

Phase Two: The Second Storm of Grief: Often occurring around six months after a death, the second storm is a time of renewed deep pain. This phase of grief may seem unbearable, and you may even wonder if you will survive the storm.

Phase Three: The Search for Meaning: Eventually, you start to shape a new and meaningful life despite your loss. Sometimes during this phase you may even feel gratitude for lessons learned on the journey.

Since grief is not a linear process, these phases often overlap. Adults, for example, may grapple with painful feelings while still denying that the death ever happened, or may discover a

new purpose in life even while dealing with painful or unresolved memories. And children may struggle with the pain of a
loss before they are fully capable of understanding the concept
of death.

Grief Does Not Come with an Expiration Date

It was Robert Benchley who said, "Death ends a life, not a relationship." Learning to go on after loss often means rethinking
your relationship with the one who has died. For many, both
adults and children, religious belief contributes to the ability to
think of the dead in heaven or in some other celestial context.
For others, the dead hold a place in their hearts, which inspires
them to live well in their memory.

Even once you have made peace with your loss, you may still
experience surges of painful grief, called triggers. These may occur on anniversary dates, like birthdays and dates of death, or
(even many years after a death) during significant life transitions:
high school graduation, marriage, births of children and grand-
children, divorce, retirement. Sometimes, too, the dead return in
waking visions, in dreams, or in other seemingly unexplainable
ways. The old notion of needing to let go and move on as quickly
as possible after a death may no longer be as relevant as establishing ongoing relationships with those who have died. No matter
what age you are when the loss occurs, grief may actually be a
lifelong process. And perhaps, when someone you cared for deeply
has died, it should be.

Preparing for the Journey That Lies Ahead

Grief is tough for everyone; it's even more difficult when you are also concerned about your child or children. This book will help you to prepare for the great journey ahead of you, and to take heart knowing that you and your child have much to gain by walking together, hand in hand.

∞ 2 ∞

Your Child Is Grieving, Too

Children have been misunderstood grievers for too long. Many people assume that since they're just kids, they don't understand, and anyway, children are so resilient, right? It *is* easy to conclude that children don't grieve. If a six-year-old wants to go to the playground after his father's funeral, he certainly appears to have gotten over it already. When a teenager completes her college application on time, even though the deadline was one week after her brother's death, she may not seem to be grieving at all. Don't be deceived by appearances. Despite how he or she behaves, your child is grieving in his or her own unique way. While you may be experiencing your loss quite differently from your child, you both share something profound.

Expand Your Comfort Zone Around Death

Few of us can say we grew up in homes where death hadn't caused a major disruption in life or was so easily accepted that no one suffered. For most people, death was a subject that was not

discussed until it happened, and sometimes it was never, ever, discussed with the children in the family. This was not the case for
my friend Judith. As a young girl, each morning, rain or shine, she
and her mother took long walks together through their neighborhood. Together they did their errands, chatted with neighbors,
and walked through the park. They also always made a stop at the
neighborhood funeral home around the corner from their house,
just to see if anyone they knew had died. As they approached the
funeral home, her mother cheerfully said to her, "Okay, Judy, let's
see who died today!" The subject of death was simply part of
their everyday routine, and when later it personally touched their
lives, they had already laid the groundwork for honest talk and
mutual support.

Families like Judith's are rare. Most of us grew up in homes
where it was assumed that kids needed to be protected against bad
things, and that not sharing grief with them was the right thing to
do. If adults believed that children grieved at all, they didn't know
how to talk to anyone about it, let alone children. Many parents
assumed that children did not grieve, or they misread cues and believed that because their kids were not showing grief as an adult
would, it wasn't there.

We now know differently. Children do grieve, and they need
our help getting through it. Unfortunately, however, death in
our culture is often a taboo subject, and when death occurs,
many families still treat kids the way they were always treated in
the past.

Face Your Bereavement Learning Curve

If, during your own childhood, you felt abandoned by your
parents after a death in your family, then it should come as no

surprise that you are now uncomfortable talking about death with your own child, and that you don't know where to begin. If you fall into this category, it helps to know that you are not alone. Many adults are uncertain about how to be available to their children at times of great loss. In fact, we all have a lot to learn about adult grief in particular, and about childhood grief in general, in order to help our families heal. The learning curve is not only an issue for you as a parent, but for those you go to for help as well. Sadly, many helping professionals have little or no training in treating grieving adults or children. For this reason, before turning to any helping professional, make sure you ask about his or her comfort and expertise when it comes to grief and loss. In Part Five, we'll explore how to find competent bereavement professionals when you need them. However, whether or not you think you need professional support, knowing your child needs your help with his grief should motivate you to learn how to deal with your own grief as well.

Dangers and Opportunities When Children Grieve

Embedded in the Chinese word for crisis are two seemingly divergent ideas: danger and opportunity. Because there are serious risks and dangers for bereaved young people who are not supported by caring adults, this concept of danger and opportunity coexisting is particularly apropos when it comes to childhood and adolescent grief. Let's consider the risks according to specific age groups:

- **Preverbal youngsters:** Even very young children sense that something terrible has happened when a death occurs. If you ignore their grief, they will miss the comfort and care you can provide.

- **Two- to five-year-olds:** When these children are not given clear information, they draw their own, often erroneous, conclusions, developing unnecessary fears about what has happened and why.
- **Six- to nine-year-olds:** Children of this age group are likely to be concerned about their own safety and the safety of family members. If not helped to manage their grief, they may worry needlessly, act out, or isolate themselves from others.
- **Ten- to twelve-year-olds:** These children often ask for lots of nitty-gritty details about death. While this is normal, if you're not aware of the idiosyncrasies of this age group, their typically persistent curiosity may come across as inappropriate, or even cruel. If this is the case, adult discomfort with their behavior may lead to their getting short shrift when it comes to their feelings being supported.
- **Teens:** Many teens often have trouble managing strong emotions. If left to their own devices, they may act out aggressively toward others, or withdraw and turn inward. Feeling alone, confused, and misunderstood, they (and younger children as well) may be at risk of misusing alcohol, experimenting with illegal and dangerous substances, hurting themselves by cutting parts of their bodies, developing eating disorders, or even attempting suicide.

In addition to dangers, there are also opportunities when death touches the lives of children. This is especially true when parents and other loving adults provide the necessary supports. Again and again, I have met bereaved children and teens who, having had caring adults who supported them, came away from their losses stronger, more self-aware, and more engaged in the world. They also had a deep appreciation for what it means to give and receive compassionate care. Throughout this book you will be introduced to many of these young people, as well as the adults in their lives who learned how to understand and assist them in their grief.

I strongly believe that one of the best things you can do for your youngster is to acknowledge that your whole family is grieving together. Parts Two and Three of this book will teach you how to walk the journey of grief and loss with your child by embracing feelings even as you learn how to help your child. Grieving hand in hand with your child, you will provide the loving care and understanding he or she needs to thrive in the face of death. Despite the pain and sorrow you and your child are feeling, you can teach your child that even the most difficult emotions and reactions to loss are manageable, and especially that despite deep loss, life can and does go on and hope can be restored.

PART TWO

EMBARKING ON THE JOURNEY

∞ 3 ∞

The First Grief Phase:
Early Grief

Whether a death is sudden or expected, we often start our grieving in a state of shock. Even with time to get ready, to deal with unfinished business, and to say good-bye, we're often left unprepared for the absolute finality of death itself. This profoundly disconcerting period, called early grief, is a time when we're struggling to face what seems absolutely unthinkable. This chapter will address three common reactions during early grief: denial of fact, anxiety, and numbness.

Denial of Fact

Grief can be crazy making. While intellectually you know a death has occurred, on another level you don't believe it's true. We typically begin grieving with a denial: "No! This is impossible. It can't be true!" And you may indeed find yourself in this state of absolute, irrational disbelief. The time frame of early grief varies, and sometimes, as in the example below, extraordinary circumstances keep us in this early response period for quite a long time.

During a morning break at one of my seminars, a woman shared with me that she had been struggling with a kind of immobilizing disbelief for three years. When I asked her what had happened, she explained that both her husband and her son had been murdered three years earlier. Understandably, the trauma of two violent and shocking deaths, followed by the drama of a prolonged and public trial, kept her in a state of denial longer than most of us ever have to endure. Only after the trials associated with the deaths of her husband and son were over could she finally move beyond early grief. (Later in this book we'll examine challenges that families face when deaths are traumatic or violent.)

More typically, denial of fact can last hours, days, sometimes even months during early grief. This is normal, and is often a very effective way of managing the news when something terrible has happened.

Denial during early grief manifests itself in various ways. For instance, it would be normal to find yourself dialing your loved one's phone number, thinking you see him in a crowd of people, or believing you hear her car pull into the driveway. You may also wonder if you are in the middle of a bad dream, and that when you finally awake you'll return to the world you once knew.

Perhaps the reason so many of us experience denial in early grief is because we need time to grasp the immensity of the loss in our lives. To take in all the ramifications at once would be too difficult, so denial allows us to look at what has happened in small, more palatable doses. However, denial does become problematic if it starts interfering with some of the normal challenges that you face during early grief. For instance, there are usually a slew of decisions to make and actions you need to take: choosing a funeral home, deciding whether to bury or cremate your loved one, and designing funeral or memorial services, to name a few. After denial kicks in, it sometimes becomes difficult to move into this more active, decision-making mode typically required of us in early grief.

If you are feeling immobilized, it is important to remember that you don't have to do everything alone, that there is often no better time than now to lean on your loved ones. As you move in and out of denial during early grief, consider calling on trusted family members and dear friends to assist you. Time and time again I've seen grievers start to take necessary actions during early grief once their family and friends have joined them on the journey.

There are times, however, when extraordinary circumstances separate you from those you need and love—you may be far from home as you face your loss; or perhaps a disaster has scattered your friends and family and left you and your child to face your loss alone. If circumstances make it difficult or impossible for you to connect with the people you would otherwise count on for support, then I urge you to contact a hospice in your area and request their support services. Hospices are committed to bringing people together during early grief, regardless of whether or not they cared for your loved one. Hospice bereavement support services are typically free, and bereavement coordinators and volunteers are available to help you.

There are so many ways that hospice support can make a difference. In Biloxi, Mississippi, a hospice team invited me to facilitate support groups after Hurricanes Katrina and Rita had devastated their city. As I toured the city, I saw homeless people roaming barren streets where houses and stores once stood. A large tent city had formed amid the ruins in one downtown neighborhood. Thousands of residents were separated from loved ones and many survivors of the storms were scattered for hundreds, even thousands of miles. The entire city was grieving, but I suspect that those who established some semblance of a community connection fared much better than those who did not. In one support group that I facilitated, all group members were homeless, dealing with a whole range of serious losses. They huddled together in a church parlor and shared their stories.

A retired minister and his wife had recently relocated from Minneapolis, to build their dream house in Biloxi. Their house had washed away in the storm. Now they were strangers in a city in ruins. They were impatient with each other and angry with God for their misfortune.

A young married couple were trying to make the best of their new makeshift home, a tiny, claustrophobic FEMA trailer standing alongside the foundation of the washed-away structure that was once their house. A friend had just died, struck by a collapsed beam at his home. They had no family, and none of their other friends remained in Biloxi. Before Katrina, the husband was physically disabled with a back injury and the wife suffered with debilitating anxiety, but they had always found work under the table and could make ends meet. Now they were penniless. "All we have now," she said to the group, "is our love for each other." It didn't seem enough to them, and they were desperate.

A Vietnam veteran and his Cambodian wife had worked for many years together at a large casino now demolished in the storm. He told the group how, as the water in their home rose, he tied his wife to his back and swam out through a window and onto dry land. While swimming to safety, they saw their neighbor floating dead in the water. During the group session his wife recalled how, long ago in Cambodia, her home had been destroyed in a typhoon and many loved ones had died. Now, in America, she was frightened, homeless, and bereaved once again.

A single woman could barely speak. She described how the debilitating flashbacks of death and destruction she was suffering interfered with her ability to concentrate at work. She feared she would be fired from her job.

An elderly African-American woman was the last to speak. She told how she'd always been proud of her self-reliance, especially since her husband's death a year earlier. Now she was living alone in a tent outside her demolished home, depressed and physically exhausted. Her children, displaced by the storm and living in Houston, were trying to hold their own families together. They were too far away to help their mother in Biloxi, and she was ashamed of herself for needing them.

After everyone had shared their stories, there was silence. Then the disabled young man sitting with his wife rose from his chair and walked over to the older African-American woman. He reached out to her and gently wrapped his arms around her. Everyone stood up to join them in a long and silent group embrace. A new community had been formed. Later, cell phone numbers were exchanged and plans were made to meet again.

You don't have to remain isolated. Like the group members in Biloxi, if your normal support network is unavailable to you at the moment, hospice and other community resources can help you muster up the strength you'll need right now to face the reality of your loss. In Part Five of this book, you'll learn how to find hospice and other bereavement supports near where you live.

Anxiety

High anxiety often occurs alongside denial. When I worked with doctors and nurses delivering bad news in the emergency room and ICUs of a large medical center, I saw all sorts of anxiety reactions. I remember walking with a physician into the waiting room outside the pediatric ICU to tell a completely unsuspecting woman, only one hour after her son had been admitted to the hospital with "just a fever," that her son was dead. Her disbelief and terror were palpable. She started to scream, and with remarkable strength, lifted heavy wooden tables and chairs over her head and threw them around the room. A wise nurse called the woman's husband, who rushed over to the hospital. He found the doctor and me in a corner, nervously eyeing his wife, who was still out of control. Approaching her calmly, he waited until their eyes met. Then a deep, guttural groan emanated from them as they embraced, dropped to the floor, and wept together. Not every grieving person acts out violently, but all of us have intense feelings that can be just as paralyzing and intimidating.

Some other common reactions during early grief include deep sadness, fear, confusion, forgetfulness, fatigue, irritability, longing, and loneliness. In addition, you may have one or many of these symptoms: a lack of energy, headaches, backaches, muscle tremors, dizziness, digestive problems, tightness in your chest or throat, and a greater than usual sensitivity to noise in your environment. Appetite changes and erratic sleep are also common reactions in early grief. Think of these reactions as your emotional and physical responses to an unthinkable circumstance in your life. They are all normal reactions. Grief is exhausting and very hard work, and you have only just begun to grasp the magnitude of what has happened.

Numbness

For some people, the reaction is delayed. Instead, a numbness sometimes comes very soon after learning of a death. While this is normal, you may feel odd and uncomfortable as you realize the absence of any emotions. In two examples below, early grievers were disturbed that they seemed to have no emotional reactions. They found it helpful, though, to learn that numbness is normal and feelings would emerge in their own time.

At the deathbed of her husband, one woman whispered to me in a small, childlike voice, "I feel nothing. What am I supposed to feel now?" I told her that it was okay to have no feelings at all, and that some feelings might show up a little later on. A few weeks later when we spoke on the phone, she told me that for the first several days after leaving the hospital, she clung to my words because they helped her feel more normal and begin to trust herself.

At a bereavement seminar, a participant recalled that for the first year after her husband's death she had no feelings, and that even ten years later, she was still ashamed and felt inadequate as a widow, even though many feelings *had* surfaced after the one-year anniversary of her husband's death. Like the woman I met in the ICU, she revealed that it was a relief just knowing that she was not nearly as odd as she felt she was and that her reaction was normal.

If you are feeling numb right now, take comfort in knowing that this is a common way of processing our losses early on. Be patient. Sometimes numbness occurs later during early grief, after a period of intense feeling. This is also quite common, and is often followed by a rather shocking resurfacing of deep pain bursting forth, seemingly out of the numbness. Some refer to this rather disconcerting yet normal phenomenon as "the calm before the storm." In the anecdote below, Sue was able to sense that painful reactions were soon to come.

My client, Sue, started working with me after her eight-year-old daughter died of leukemia. While she had many intense early feelings, about four months into our work together, she reported noticing an absence of any feelings at all. I'll never forget what she said to me during a session:

"I don't know what it is, but I can feel something changing. This numbness is only temporary, I'm sure. I can't quite explain it, but I know it's going to be extremely difficult and intense when the feelings come back, as if I were sticking my finger into an electric socket!"

Most of us don't have Sue's sixth sense. In fact, most grievers are alarmed by this second storm of grief that Sue felt coming. Try to remember that while it is easy for numbness to lull you into believing that your grief has ended and that the worst of your grief is over, your grief will probably reappear in full force. Later, in Part Three, we'll explore this second storm of grief that typically follows early grief. For now, take comfort in knowing that a delayed reaction and numbness in early grief are quite common. Perhaps they provide ways that enable you to take your loss in small, more palatable doses. Whether your reactions have been overwhelming, hidden, or something in between, remember to trust that your feelings will emerge at the right time for you.

In summary, denial, anxiety, and numbness often come with the territory when grief is new. If this has been your experience, consider the following suggestions of what to do when your grief is very new.

Reach Out to Others: Grief can be immobilizing, especially when it is new, so start gathering your support network. Right now you need friends, family, or other support people close by to help you face what is happening and take necessary action.

Cultivate Your Strengths: As you face the unthinkable, you might lose sight of your unique strengths. It is normal to be unsure as to whether you have what it takes to deal with what has happened to you.

- Ask someone you trust, someone who really knows you, to remind you how you've faced adversity well in the past.
- Gather your spiritual resources. For some, this means turning to a trusted clergyperson or having a conversation with a hospital or hospice chaplain. For others, it may involve listening to inspirational music, practicing meditation, or watching the sunrise and sunset.
- Do small tasks that can be completed with success. Even doing the laundry or mending something that needs to be fixed can leave you with a sense of competence and accomplishment.

Grappling with Your Anxiety

Have you ever felt this way before? If so, how did you cope? What did you learn about anxiety then that can help you now? There are many effective ways to deal with anxiety. I often think of coping strategies for anxiety on a continuum, from meditation to medication. Certainly medication can be an effective way to manage overwhelming anxiety, but you might also consider guided relaxation tapes, meditation, prayer, listening to soothing music, taking a warm bath, and physical exercise. Have a conversation with a trusted friend or professional about various anxiety-reducing strategies. (In Part Five you'll find suggestions for help if anxiety continues to overwhelm you.)

Once you have begun to meet the challenges of your own early grief, you will be better prepared to start helping your youngster understand the meaning and the cause of the death that has touched your lives. The next chapter will explore how to walk with your child during early grief.

4

How to Tell Your Child
What Has Happened

As you struggle to make sense of the tragedy that has just occurred, remember that your child is also trying to understand what has happened. One of the most common reasons why children fail to comprehend the meaning of death is that their parents don't offer clear and concrete information. By breaking down the task at hand into manageable steps, you will be able to handle this difficult challenge, even while you are grieving. This chapter will help you consider the most effective language to use when you explain death to your child.

Your Feelings First

Before we go any further, let's consider your feelings again. What if you were to cry in front of your child? As a grief counselor, I am privy to many tragic stories of loss. Sometimes I am moved to tears, and usually that serves my clients well. Of course, we must always listen to the subtle and not-so-subtle messages children send us. I remember how, in my first session with Paul, a savvy young teenager dealing with a series of tragedies, he strutted into my office, sat right down, and the very first words out of his mouth were "My last therapist cried. Don't cry!"

So here are three thoughts about crying: First, if you cry in front of your child, perhaps you are allowing your child to see that you are comfortable with your feelings. Second, when you cry, you are giving permission to your child to cry as well. And third, be careful not to overwhelm your child. Sometimes our feelings can be disturbing to young people. This was how Paul clearly felt about his former therapist's tears. I told Paul that I appreciated his honesty and that I would do my best to manage my sadness, but since people can't always control their feelings, if I were to cry, I'd definitely want to talk about it with him.

We show our feelings in all sorts of ways to our kids, and, for the most part, this is good. If you don't know how your child feels about seeing you cry, then ask her about it. If it is frightening or making her uncomfortable, tell her that you are okay and that she doesn't have to take care of you.

How Adults Understand Death

Here are some basic concepts that help grief professionals comprehend how adults understand death:

- When a person dies we mean that the body has totally stopped working.
- The dead cannot return to life.
- Someday we will all die.

Although these concepts may seem pretty straightforward, we all have different ways of understanding them. Some factors that contribute to this difference are religion, spiritual beliefs, ethnic and cultural practices, and personal experiences. It would be worthwhile to ask yourself the following questions before talking to your child about death:

- Does the idea that death means that the body has stopped working get more complicated for you if a person is in a persistent vegetative state or is declared brain dead?
- If you believe in heaven, does your belief affect your notion of death as irreversible?
- How do your behaviors support your belief that everyone dies? For instance, do you wear a seat belt, exercise regularly, and take proper precautions when participating in high-risk sports?

Understanding the three concepts is much more complicated for children than for adults. One reason why children have difficulty understanding them is that too often grown-ups are not adequately clear and concrete when explaining death to children. For instance, most adults use code words (*passed away, passed on, resting peacefully, lost, kicked the bucket*, etc.) for death. When children hear us referring to death indirectly, they can get very confused or even frightened. Consider being more direct by actually using the word *dead* when you talk to your child.

How to Clearly Define Death to Your Child

The clearest definition I've found for being dead is simply that the person's body has totally stopped working. For children younger than age five or six, try being even more specific: "Her eyes don't see, her ears don't hear, her brain can't think or remember. She can no longer feel pain or have any other sensations, her body can't do things, and she no longer has to go to the bathroom. She no longer has feelings. Everything has stopped working."

If you believe in heaven, be clear to your child about what your concept of heaven is and talk about it right after you explain that the body is now dead. Here, the order in which you discuss these issues is very important. First, explain what it means to be dead, and *then* explain heaven. If you skip over the death explanation and go right to heaven, children are likely to be confused and to think of heaven as a wonderful place to go while they're still alive. They may become so confused that they want to visit their loved one in heaven or call her on the phone and beg her to come back home.

How to Explain the Cause of a Death

Children also need help understanding the cause of death. Whether it is cancer, AIDS, or some another illness or an accidental death or a homicide or suicide, it is important that children receive appropriate information to help them begin to understand. If we don't give them clear information, they may manufacture their own explanations and become unnecessarily frightened. For instance, they may believe that a particular illness is contagious when, in fact, it is not. If their imaginations take hold, they may struggle with unnecessary fears that they or other members of their family would be at risk of falling ill and/or dying, too. Three principles will be helpful when you prepare to explain the cause of death to your child.

1. Don't try to say everything at once. Instead, say only what you believe is essential for your child to know.
2. Let your child set the pace of the conversation. Sometimes children have a lot of questions, but other times they want

information in very small doses, and would prefer switching to another topic of conversation entirely, or would like to go to the mall, or eat lunch.

3. When possible, take time to prepare for the conversation with your child. For instance, consider asking a friend or counselor to role-play some conversations with you first.

You don't have to do this alone; ask a trusted friend or family member to join you. Remember, the more prepared you are, the less anxious you and your child will be.

In the following example, only hours after her husband's suicide, Mary was faced with having to tell her eight-year-old son that his father had died. She first chose appropriate language so that her son would have the most "necessary" information, then she listened carefully to her son's reaction in order to know how to appropriately pace the conversation, and finally, she found someone she could collaborate with for the long, difficult journey ahead.

Mary found her husband at home, dead from a self-inflicted gunshot wound. As she recovered from her own shock and disbelief, she realized how grateful she was that her eight-year-old son was not with her and was spared the trauma of finding his dead father. Initially, as she formulated her plan of action, she hoped to hide the suicide story from her son. Then she realized that if she didn't tell him, he'd eventually hear about it at school or on the news. Unsure as to how to proceed, she called some friends for help and, eventually, got my phone number. By the time we talked, Mary was ready to tell her son that his father had killed himself, but still she had no idea where to begin. I coached her over the phone, and that evening, her conversation with the boy went something like this:

"Daddy died. That means that his body totally stopped working. He died from suicide. A suicide death is when someone makes his body stop working." She paused and asked the boy, "What more would you like to know?"

First, Mary explained the suicide story in its simplest terms: "Daddy made his body stop working." Then she paced the conversation by letting her son choose what he wanted to do next.

If her son didn't ask any more questions and wanted to end the conversation, I told Mary to sit a little while longer with him and make a list of the safest grown-ups he could turn to if he had questions later. I also told her to prepare for two questions that were likely to come up sooner or later: How and Why.

How Did It Happen?: If he were to ask how, I told Mary to use the least overwhelming language possible. She eventually told him that his daddy made his body stop working with a gun. The entire story was much more graphic, but she used the least overwhelming, yet truthful, explanation.

Why Did It Happen?: I suggested to Mary that if she didn't know why, it would be perfectly fine to admit this to her son. But if she suspected that the suicide was the result of a mental illness, even a young child can understand that a mental illness can cause great pain, which sometimes leads to suicide. I also advised Mary to tell her child about alternatives to suicide, such as professional counseling, group support, medication, and hospitalization.

In Chapter Seventeen, we'll look in greater depth at some of the challenges associated with traumatic deaths, like suicides and homicides, and how you can find resources to support yourself and your child, but regardless of the cause of death, it is very troubling for most adults to tell children things that will ultimately be frightening and difficult to live with. Nevertheless, by honoring your own feelings, remembering to use honest, simple, and concrete language, and patiently pacing parent-child conversations, you will become the resource your child desperately needs during this difficult time.

WHAT TO REMEMBER

You Are Now a Family in Grief Together

Your child will not only be learning from what you say, but also by how he or she sees you managing your own feelings. There may very well be times, as you and your child grieve together, that you find yourself so overwhelmed that you are unable to be the parent you wish to be. For this reason, too often bereaved children of all ages get short shrift as they grieve. For instance, bereaved siblings often describe how they not only lost a brother or sister, but also one or both of their parents just when they needed them most. One bereaved mother revealed to me that she was so overwhelmed after her son's death that she had no idea that her other teenager had become suicidal as he grieved. As disturbing as this is, I believe strongly that with proper attention to your own process and to the needs of your children, your family can safely weather the storm.

First, I urge you to frankly assess what you need to do for yourself, and then determine what your children will need in the meantime. For instance, a widow told me that for several months after her husband's death she was unable to get out of bed to help her ten- and eleven-year-old children get ready for school. She took the bull by the horns, sat them down, and explained that grief sometimes is so exhausting that even grown-ups need a lot more rest than usual. Lately, she explained to them, she'd been so tired that she needed to stay in bed in the morning. She reassured them that this would only be temporary, and in the meantime, she arranged for a trusted neighbor to stop in each morning to prepare breakfast and make sure they got to the bus stop. Over time, as she became able to take on more and more of her usual parenting responsibilities, her children began to learn that while their lives had been altered irrevocably by their father's death, their mother was taking care of herself *and* seeing to it that they would always be well cared for, too.

This Is Not the Only Conversation You and Your Child Will Have

Think about this as the beginning of a lifelong process of learning to understand what has happened. Tell your child that not even grown ups can always understand or manage all of their feelings just by talking about it once, and that lots of large feelings take time, patience, love, and hard work to understand and manage well.

Children have different needs at different ages, too. Children of all ages, including teens, need nurturing, information, and support as they grieve. In the next chapter we'll look more closely at how your child's needs and concerns will change as he or she advances through some predictable developmental stages.

5

Developmental Challenges
for Children and Teens

This chapter addresses some common developmental factors that can interfere with a child's ability to understand the basic concepts of death that were addressed in the last chapter: first, that a dead body has completely stopped functioning; second, that a person who dies will not return; and third, that every living thing will eventually die. As you read this chapter, remember that as your child moves through the different developmental stages, she'll discover a deeper, more mature understanding of these three concepts. Developmental stages, while critically important for you to know about, are based on generalizations. Not every child experiences his or her grief according to the descriptions below. Nonetheless, I encourage you to read about all five of the developmental stages of childhood and adolescence. Children often regress to earlier stages of development during a crisis, so even if your child is older, she may struggle with issues more commonly found among younger kids. In addition, if you have more than one child, this information will help you appreciate their different concerns. As your child matures and advances through the developmental stages, the information in this chapter will help you prepare for some of the changes to come. Before we go any further, let's review some general concerns children face within each developmental stage:

- **Preverbal children** can sense when there is a crisis in their families, and while they can't express themselves verbally, they may understand something about their loss. Be on the lookout for nonverbal clues that they understand more than is easily apparent.
- **Two- to five-year-olds** need to be given clear, concise information in order to keep them from drawing erroneous conclusions about what has happened and why.
- **Six- to nine-year-olds** are likely to be concerned about their own safety and the safety of others in their families
- **Ten- to twelve-year-olds** are very curious and often seek out lots of details about a death.
- **Adolescents** often have trouble managing their strong emotions, may experience survivor guilt after a death, and, if left to their own devices, may act out aggressively toward others, or retreat and turn inward.

Now we can move forward and take a closer look at each of the developmental stages.

Preverbal Children

Since these are the youngest members of the family, we could easily assume they don't experience any grief at all. While it is true that preverbal children don't fully grasp any of the three foundational concepts, they may still surprise us with a depth of understanding following a death that belies their young age. As you read this next anecdote, notice how Pat came to realize that her daughter, Carla, was demonstrating her grief nonverbally.

Pat and her infant daughter moved into the children's unit of a hospital the last few weeks in the life of Pat's son, Tito. Little Carla slept alongside her brother while Pat stretched out to catch a few winks on a recliner pulled up beside the two youngsters. Carla was playing with LEGOs in her brother's hospital room when Tito died. Understandably, Pat assumed that Carla didn't understand what had happened, and that she certainly wouldn't grieve his death. A week after Tito's death, Pat came into my office to talk.

"When Carla and I got home after Tito died, all I could do was hold my little girl in my arms and weep. I squeezed her close to me, paced around my apartment for hours, and we cried and cried. For the longest time, I assumed that Carla was just crying because I was and that an infant couldn't possibly grieve. But after a few days of this, something remarkable occurred. As I carried her and we wept together, I noticed that whenever I walked past the picture of Tito in the hallway, Carla reached over and pointed to the picture, and cried even harder. I finally realized that my baby understood more than I ever imagined possible!"

It would have been easy for Pat to assume that Carla was merely acting cranky, but being an extraordinarily observant person, she was able to realize that her daughter was actually expressing her own grief by pointing to her brother's picture and crying.

If you have a preverbal youngster at home, remember these three suggestions: First, provide gentle, nurturing physical touch. Second, speak to her using simple, feeling-focused language, such as "We're so sad." Third, offer concrete, affirming, basic explanations of death, such as "We are so sad because your brother died. His body totally stopped working."

Two- to Five-Year-Olds

Similar to preverbal children, two- to five-year-olds don't easily grasp the three foundational concepts: that the body stops working, you don't come back, and all living things die. So be prepared to repeat explanations to your child. Children at this age tend to ask a lot of questions over and over again, like "When is Mommy coming back?" or "How can she breath when the casket is closed?" Such questions reflect the child's inability to grasp basic concepts that we adults more easily associate with being dead. Regardless of this difference, you can still find opportunities to go to a deeper, feeling-focused level with your child. For example, in this next anecdote, Cory's kindergarten teacher felt frustrated by Cory's inability to comprehend that the dead do not ever return, but finally realized that even if death was something Cory could not yet fully understand, he could still be helped to express and share sad feelings and meaningful memories.

Dr. Connors, a beloved elementary school principal, had died suddenly. This death was particularly difficult since Dr. Connors was an exceptionally caring and involved principal who had established very close bonds with children, faculty, and parents. Every morning, rain or shine, he stood in the school parking lot and greeted each child by name, and he always met weekly with each classroom in his school, where he read a chapter book, told a story, or recited poetry. After his death, Cory stood at the doorway to his classroom and waited for his teacher to notice him there. She joined him at the doorway and they would walk together into class and over to a picture of Dr. Connors that hung on the wall in the back of the room. Cory looked at the picture for a moment, and then turned longingly to his teacher and asked her, "Is he coming back *today*?" Each day, she explained that Dr. Connors was dead and wouldn't be coming back to school anymore. This went on for weeks. Finally, Cory's teacher decided to focus on feelings instead of trying to explain a concept to Cory that kept eluding him. The next morning, when Cory asked her if Dr. Connors would be coming back, she put her arm around him and said, "I really miss Dr. Connors, too." They cried together, and then she helped him find the words to express his feelings. Later on, during a class meeting, the children were invited to talk about some of the things they missed about Dr. Connors. They also decided to implement some new school rituals in his memory.

By sharing her own sad feelings with her student, Cory's teacher created an opportunity for grief to be processed despite Cory's developmental block. Try this approach with your child if you get caught up in a similar cycle of repeated questions about concepts that are beyond your child's ability to understand.

Although developmental limitations can cause serious challenges for two- to five-year-olds, there are often practical solutions. In Chapter Four, you learned how to explain that being dead means that the body totally stops working. However, since children at this age often have difficulty mastering this concept, the mere closing of a casket can trigger all sorts of fears. If your child worries about how a loved one will fare in the casket, and if simple explanations about being dead aren't enough to soothe your child's concerns, perhaps you both could put a letter or drawings or even a flashlight inside the casket, if she worries that the person who died would be afraid of the dark inside the casket. If you do this, remember to explain to your child that the dead don't need these gifts, but sometimes those of us who grieve need to feel as though we're helping them.

Six- to Nine-Year-Olds

Children in this age group have a particularly tough time understanding that death is universal. They tend to personify death as an evil spirit or bogeyman that can't catch you as long as you can run fast enough. Therefore, they're likely to believe that only the extremely aged, the severely handicapped, and the seriously clumsy ever really die, while the rest of us will always escape death entirely. However, if someone they had once believed to be safe from death actually *does* die, then the child's whole world suddenly begins to look terribly unpredictable and insecure. You don't have to scratch too deeply to hear such concerns as "What happens to *me* if my mommy or daddy dies?" "Who will take me to school?" "Who will make the money?" "Who will make me dinner?" "Who will tuck me in at night?" In this next story, you'll meet eight-year-old Sid, who at first was very anxious when his parents planned to take a vacation without him, until they assured him that they would look after his needs, even in the unlikely event they were to die.

Sid's special aunt and his best friend's father both died in the same year. Now each time his parents planned a romantic getaway without him, Sid became inconsolable. Merely reassuring him that they would return wasn't comforting enough for him and, unfortunately, they had to cancel two trips. Since Sid had lived through two deaths already, he knew very well that all of his parents' efforts to reassure him that nothing would happen to them wouldn't prevent random tragedies from happening again. For this reason, Sid needed to know that he would be taken care of in the event that something *did* happen to his parents. His parents made out a will, appointed a guardian, and talked to Sid about what they had done. Now Sid understands that although his parents strongly believe they will return safely from their weekend away, they've also made arrangements so that, in the unlikely event that something does happen to them, Sid will be taken care of. Sid is convinced now that his parents have considered all contingencies, and he is ready to let them go on vacations without him.

By writing your will and establishing guardianship plans, your child, like Sid, will hopefully become convinced that you'll always be looking out for her. Still, it would not be unusual for your child to have started worrying excessively about losing you or other important people in her life. Perhaps she would find more comfort if you explained to her that while every life will end someday, there is some predictability to this, and that this predictability is known as life expectancy. If you believe you have a good chance of living a long life, then tell your child that you have every reason to believe that you'll live into your eighties or nineties, or even longer, and tell her about others in the family who have lived good long lives, too. I never agree with parents lying to their children, saying that they needn't worry because parents never die. That would be foolish and is guaranteed to backfire someday. Instead, if your six- to nine-year-old child is grieving, tell her that while it is true that everyone will someday die—even people she needs and loves—most people live long lives. A list of books that can help you explain these important concepts to your child can be found at the back of this volume.

Ten- to Twelve-Year-Olds

By the time children reach age nine or ten, they have typically mastered the three foundational concepts that being dead means the body has totally stopped working, the dead don't return, and all living things die. While understanding death tends to generate all sorts of painful feelings in most people, these school-aged children tend to react differently. In this next anecdote a couple needed my reassurance when they saw children in this age group not exhibiting any emotions at a wake.

Ellen and June's twelve-year-old daughter and several cousins of the same age were attending a cousin's wake, when suddenly they all seemed to disappear. After a time, many parents became concerned, especially when an informal search party couldn't find the children anywhere in the funeral home or on the grounds. It turned out the kids were hanging out with one of the funeral directors in the embalming room, asking all sorts of questions about embalming and preparing a body for showing in an open casket.

Although these children seemed strangely insensitive, their concerns are typical for their age group. Ten- to twelve-year-olds tend to grieve more in their heads and less in their hearts. While Ellen and June were surprised to hear this, they were also quite relieved to learn that their daughter was normal. You may find that there is an element of insensitivity to your child at this age. She wants to know more about the facts and is much less oriented to her feelings. For instance, a boy once sidled up to his grieving mother, put his arm around her, looked into her eyes, and asked, "So how long before Daddy's body decomposes?" This was not what his mother wanted to think about or talk about to anyone. If your youngster challenges you with questions and comments that take your breath away, remember that your child's interests and concerns are very normal. Take a deep breath, and then decide how you can steer your child in the right direction to get the information she desires. The list of books in the back of this volume can help you with this age group and its challenges.

Adolescents

Teens tend to be much more feeling-focused grievers than ten- to twelve-year-olds. While they understand the three foundational concepts, teens are often confused with the notion of universality and are likely to try to defy death, as if to say "This can't happen to *us*!" But when death does intrude into their social sphere, teens tend to grapple with survivor guilt, high anxiety, and a whole range of difficult emotions, and often don't know where to turn. Of course, not all teenagers respond so intensely to their losses. Some are less emotional and some delay their grief in order to accomplish more pressing developmental needs, such as finding a job or applying to college. In this next story, a guidance counselor at a large inner-city vocational high school realized, when she scratched the surface, how pervasive teen grief was at her school.

One of her students, a single parent of a newborn, had been absent from school because her baby had drowned while she was bathing her. The young mother's five best girlfriends were crying inconsolably in the counselor's office.

The counselor decided to explore the idea of offering a grief support group, believing there were other grieving students in the school. She put up signs around the school to announce a brief informational meeting for anyone considering grief support, and was surprised when nearly fifty boys and girls crowded the meeting room. One by one, they told of friends and family members who had died from accidents, illnesses including cancer and AIDS, suicides, and several homicides. Due to the tremendous response from the students, she decided to sponsor both a general grief support group and a specialized homicide support group.

If you're willing to really listen to teens, you will learn that their emotional needs can be huge. Part Three looks at ways to help teenagers manage overwhelming feelings, and helps parents discern when a teenager's grief reaction requires professional attention.

WHAT TO REMEMBER

As children grow up, they face unique grieving challenges. From infancy through the young adult years, your child needs you to:
- Listen to her fears and concerns.
- Clarify misunderstandings.
- Accept your child's limitations.
- Help your child find a safe haven.

As you help your child, your own grief will probably get stirred up. You may begin to feel:
- Overwhelmed by your own loss as you are called upon to repeat, over and over again, basic information about the meaning of death to your very young child.
- Repulsed, triggered, and even angry if your preteen asks seemingly inappropriate questions, like "When will Mom's body finish decomposing?"
- Abandoned by your teenager who seems self-centered and who won't share her grief with you.

Remember that your reactions are normal. Consider talking to a friend or counselor about the feelings that get stirred up inside you as your child grieves.

Continue to review the developmental concepts as your child grows older and matures. If you have more than one child at home, the information in this chapter should help you to see how differently your children understand their shared loss. As children move through the developmental stages, their appreciation for the depth of their loss changes and their grief will be renewed again and again, so be patient and don't expect perfection. Remember that just as your child advances through developmental stages and encounters significant milestones, so will you. Over time, you will undoubtedly change and grow, too. In this respect we're really not very different from our children.

∞ 6 ∞

Creating Family-Focused
Commemorations

From almost the beginning of time, rituals honoring the dead have been important to those left behind. Commemorative events like wakes, funerals, burials, and memorial services link mourners to significant religious practices and spiritual beliefs, and bring order, comfort, familiarity, and a community connection to lives that have been disrupted. In addition to traditional commemorative events, you may want to create personalized memorial rituals with your child, such as making memory books and memorial quilts. While these sorts of informal rituals are addressed in Part Four, this chapter looks at how to implement family-focused, traditional commemorative activities.

Family-Focused Traditional Commemorations

Wakes, funerals, burials, and memorial services typically occur during early grief, when mourners are struggling with denial, anxiety, and numbness. In some families children are automatically excluded from these events, while in others they are expected to attend. In either case, these occasions are usually designed for grown-ups, and if children do attend, they are supposed to behave like little adults so as not to disturb the proceedings. On the other hand, family-friendly rituals offer developmentally appropriate activities for all young people attending. The following are some examples of family-friendly funeral activities that address the needs of specific age groups of children.

FOR PREVERBAL CHILDREN AND TWO- TO FIVE-YEAR-OLDS

While you may choose to hire a babysitter and leave your child home during a funeral, perhaps if you were to include even your young child, you'd be communicating to her that she is an important member of the family. For this reason, consider informing the funeral home that there will be very young children attending and request an adjoining room for child care. Hire experienced babysitters or ask trusted members of your family if they would be willing to forgo the service and instead provide child care during the ceremony. Ask parents to bring quiet toys and stuffed animals, favorite games, art supplies, and read-aloud books, and invite them to stay with their children.

FOR SIX- TO NINE-YEAR-OLDS

Tell the funeral home there will be children at the funeral and request an adjoining room for supervised art activities and space for the children to move around. Invite trusted, child-oriented, adult family members to supervise the children, and inform all parents that they are welcome to stay with their children. Consider allowing more mature children from this age group to quietly join the service. With adult assistance and some coordination with the minister or funeral director, it may even be possible for children to share their memory books or artwork as part of the service. I've seen this done very effectively.

FOR TEN- TO TWELVE-YEAR-OLDS

These youngsters are often mature enough to participate in the main service. If, however, a young person has died and his or her school will be releasing bereaved children to attend the funeral, ask the school to insist that a parent or guardian accompany every child to the funeral, because more than likely they will require supervision and support. Advise parents to teach their children about funeral rituals, proper etiquette at funerals, and appropriate funeral attire and behavior.

FOR ADOLESCENTS

Teenagers are old enough to participate in the main event. However, if this is your teen's first funeral, remember to teach her about funeral rituals, proper etiquette at funerals, and appropriate attire. If many teens are expected to attend, talk to the minister or funeral director about the possibility of offering a preliminary service for teens earlier in the morning, before the "main event." Have adults present to offer the teens the attention and support they need.

Frequently Asked Questions About Involving Children in Traditional Rituals

What if my child doesn't want to go to the funeral?

First of all, make sure your child, regardless of age, has the information needed to make an educated decision one way or the other. Chapter Nineteen includes resources for this purpose.

If your child decides not to attend the funeral, ask why she reached that decision. Perhaps you can make her feel safer or clarify any misunderstanding. However, if she continues to desire not to attend, support her decision and find a safe, reliable family member or trusted adult friend of the family to stay with her. This will communicate to your child that she's important and loved regardless of her decision.

How can I prepare my child for attending a funeral?

There are some excellent books about funerals that you can read to your younger child. I especially like *Tell Me, Papa* by Joy and Marv Johnson. I recommend that older kids and teens read *When Dinosaurs Die* by Laurie Krasny Brown and Marc Brown. The list at the back of this book provides information on these and other recommended materials.

What if she wants to leave the church after the funeral has started?

Preverbal children and two- to five-year-olds will be watched by an adult, so there should be no problem if they want to leave the church or funeral home during the ceremony, with your permission. Older youngsters, with appropriate supervision, should be allowed to take breaks as needed.

How do I explain cremation to a young child?

Children between two and five or six years of age are not likely to fully understand that a dead body has *totally* stopped working, so the concept of cremation might be quite frightening to them. Karen Carney's *Our Special Garden: Understanding Cremation* is a coloring book for this age group that explains cremation. Before the author even mentions cremation, she introduces three important ideas:

1. Being dead means that everything stops working, including feelings.
2. After death, the soul leaves the dead body just like when a butterfly flies away, leaving behind its cocoon.
3. We don't *completely* lose those who die, because we still have special memories we can cherish.

After she makes those three points, Carney explains cremation in a way that won't frighten young children. The list at the back of this volume has information about this and other books that discuss cremation.

What if I become too upset at the funeral to take care of my child's needs?

This will not be unusual, so plan ahead. Assign a safe, grown-up "buddy," such as a favorite aunt, to stay with your child to answer questions, provide support, and leave with her if she needs a break.

Let children of any age know that, at funerals, people express all sorts of feelings and may become very, very sad. They may stay sad for a while, but eventually they start to feel better again.

Should my child look at the dead body at a wake or funeral if the person who died was very important, like a parent, grandparent, sibling, or friend?

This would not be unusual, so plan ahead. With proper preparation and support, regardless of age, most children will handle this challenge successfully, but only if prepared and allowed to decide for themselves.

I know a man who, at the age of five, was picked up by his aunt and shoved headfirst into his grandmother's casket, to kiss her good-bye. Thirty years later, he is still traumatized by this. Never insist that your child view a body, or attend a funeral, for that matter.

If the casket will be open at a funeral, tell your child about it ahead of time. I've often found that if children five years old and younger are told that the dead person's "body" will be put in a casket, they tend to misinterpret this to mean that the person who died was decapitated and that the body, without a head, will be placed in the casket. To avoid misunderstanding, carefully clarify that the entire body, head included, will be in the casket.

If your child will be attending an open-casket funeral, explain ahead of time that viewings are always optional and, if she chooses to view the body, it is proper to go up once and then be seated. If there will be a viewing either at a wake or another time prior to the funeral, most children, regardless of age, appreciate some private time with the body, *while you are present*, to say good-bye.

WHAT TO REMEMBER

Wakes, funerals, and burial and memorial services can be meaningful and rewarding events for you and your child. They typically provide spiritual and/or existential grounding and an opportunity for receiving support from trusted family members and friends. Since children also grieve, they should not be ignored during ritual events. With forethought, you can, within your own comfort zone, let your child know she is part of a loving and caring community that won't let her down during this difficult time.

- If you choose not to allow your child to attend a ritual event, remember that she still deserves to participate in an alternative one that reflects her important status as a member of the grieving family.

- Provide your child with information about traditional family death rituals so your child can make an educated choice about whether or not to attend.
- Regardless of your child's age, make sure there is an appropriate, supportive environment at your traditional ritual event.

Early grief doesn't end when the funeral is over. Often it has only just begun. Hopefully, after the funeral, friends and family members will continue to surround you with their love and care. This is what you deserve. There will, however, come a time when you and your child find yourselves summoned back to various responsibilities that were part of your life before your loss. The transition out of the insular world of acute grief into a larger, more social environment can be difficult. With this in mind, the next chapter offers specific suggestions for managing a smooth transition back to work and school.

7

Getting Back to Work
and School

Moving outside the sanctuary of your home after a loss can be excruciating. Whether you've already returned to the workplace or will be returning shortly, you may be feeling uncertain and anxious as to whether you can resume your responsibilities. For your child, returning to school, or a sports team or club, or even getting back on the school bus can be tough, too. This chapter addresses some of the challenges children and adults face as they reorient themselves to various routines, and offers specific strategies to help adults and children reenter the larger world. First we'll look at ways you can help your child return to school and other settings.

Your Child May Feel Uncertain About His or Her World

Young people often find it hard going back to the classroom, Sunday school, and extracurricular activities after a death, especially if they feel vulnerable and believe themselves to be different from everyone else. They may worry about what others would think if they were to cry in public. They may worry that others will feel sorry for them. They may feel very tired and wonder if they can get through a long school day. They may worry about meeting normal academic requirements at school. I've spoken to many children who received no support from their families or from school personnel after the death of someone close to them.

Two years after his father's suicide, Juan came to see me for our first session. The first thing he said was "I never went back to my high school the year he died," and then, "I never stepped foot in that building ever again!" Despite persistent absences Juan had somehow managed to slip through the cracks and never got caught during that first year. The next year he got himself transferred to a different high school and had to repeat his junior year. When I asked why he had gone to such lengths to avoid ever going back, his entire demeanor changed. In the voice of a much younger child, he replied, "I just didn't want everyone staring at me, that's all." Perhaps he felt too ashamed to face his peers.

Like Juan, many youngsters need direct assistance in order to figure out the best way to return. The following instructions are appropriate for any school-aged youngster. Sit down with your child and ask these questions:

When you're ready to go back, how can I help?

If she merely shrugs or mumbles "I don't know," instead of giving up, continue with the next questions.

Are you concerned about your privacy?

If your child says "yes," you can request that a guidance counselor or teacher instruct other students and staff to refrain from drawing attention to your child.

Are you hoping for support from your friends?

If your child would appreciate hugs from friends, tell a school adjustment counselor or school nurse to tell students and staff that your child would appreciate some TLC.

Have you been exhausted lately?

This would be normal. Sometimes a few half days at school can be a good way to gradually get back. Try arranging this with your child's school if your child has been very tired.

Are you worried about getting started?

Some kids like to arrive early, before the other students, so someone on staff whom they trust can help them get ready for the day. If so, arrange this with a staff member your child trusts at her school.

Are you still concerned about anything?

Some kids like to arrange time at the end of the school day with a staff member they trust to debrief before getting back on the bus or, if it's an older child, driving home or going to an after-school job.

After exploring all the questions, come up with a plan that works best for you and your child. Remember to be patient. Especially with teenagers, parents frequently make less headway in these discussions. If he refuses to talk with you, arrange a home visit by a classroom teacher, minister, or coach to help ease his way back into regular activities. In fact, more and more school crisis teams are including reentry support in their outreach plans for youngsters in crisis, and many schools now routinely send someone to meet youngsters and their parents in their homes to talk about their returning. If there is no such plan already in place for reentry assistance for your child at her school, consider sharing information in this chapter with a teacher or guidance counselor or, for that matter, with a coach or other mentor, or with a minister or youth leader.

How to Prepare Yourself to Return to Work

Returning to work isn't easy. You may face any or all of these issues:

1. Lower productivity due to stress that comes with profound loss.
2. Diminished job performance due to impaired concentration, memory loss, or numbness.
3. Damaged work relationships due to lack of interest in socializing, misunderstandings, and unresolved feelings.
4. Increased tardiness, absenteeism, and medical complaints.

Take the Time You Need Before Returning to Work

Eleven years after his daughter died of leukemia, Tony, a quality-assurance representative, recalled how his first day back on the job one week after Lisa's death was too soon for him:

"When I arrived at my office, I knew right away that I should have stayed out longer. I felt like I was walking into a subway car with everyone staring at me. I went back to my desk and tried to start working, but I couldn't find anything. I couldn't do anything. Noises really bothered me and at one point I quickly got up and turned off a radio that was blasting at the desk of one of my coworkers. He didn't say anything and I'm glad that he didn't. It had only been a week since Lisa died and so much had happened in that time. I think I was too green that day."

Clearly, Tony had returned to work too soon. He felt high strung, anxious, and overwhelmed with grief. These were all normal early grief reactions; neither his body, mind, nor spirit were prepared for life on the job. Unfortunately, in many U.S. businesses, bereavement leave policies are limited to as few as three paid days off. Still, sometimes there are creative options available, such as "flexible leave pools" where employees can contribute their unused time so the bereaved can take extended time away from work with pay. If you need more time, ask your employer about this sort of option.

Grief Often Drains Away Energy Needed for Your Job

Three years after her husband's death, Paula, a special education teacher for twenty-three years, recalled how sheer exhaustion made work seem impossible. Fortunately, her employer was generous and patient with her as she figured out how to pick up her work life once again:

"John died unexpectedly on my first day of school. For that whole first school year I didn't go to work very much at all. I just collapsed on the couch after getting the kids to school every morning. I tried going back after a few weeks, but couldn't get through a day. Luckily, since I had a lot of sick time built up, my boss suggested that I just use it, so that's what I did.

"For a long time, I thought I would have to leave the teaching profession, because I just didn't have enough left in me to give any more. When I told my boss, he [completely] understood and advised me to take a leave for half a year, and then reevaluate. So I did. By midyear, though, I felt ready to go back to my teaching job.

"Now, three years after John's death, I am really back, really there mentally, and I love my job. In fact, I never want to leave because they've been so good to me."

Periods of Dysfunction May Interfere with Your Effectiveness on the Job

Lillian liked her job as an assistant manager at a busy medical office until her husband, Roy, died. Then her anxiety started to interfere with her ability to function on the job, and her attitude at work suffered. I spoke with her three years after Roy's death:

"I went back to work about three weeks after Roy died. I was happy to get on with my normal life, but then, a month later, right in the middle of what felt like a typical phone conversation, I had my first panic attack. The room began to spin, and I thought I was going to be sick. I put the caller on hold and asked my office manager to take the call. Then I just disintegrated. I left work, went home, and cried my heart out. I resolved that I would never let that happen again because it was so inappropriate and because I believed that nobody cared, anyway. After that, I think I functioned pretty normally for about two years, but when I had to have some surgery, I began to have the panic attacks all over again. This time they were continual and forced me out of work for about three months.

"Once back at work again, I realized that my life would never return to 'normal.' I could barely get out of bed in the morning, and once I arrived at work I couldn't function at my normal level of productivity. Not only that, but I didn't want to be there and I was no longer the hardworking employee I used to be. I began to stretch out my job tasks, deliberately working really slowly. I simply showed up, put my head down, and did the minimum, *and* I would get angry with my supervisor if she asked me to do any-thing.

"Eventually, though, I learned to differentiate between reason-able requests from my supervisor and those that were simply im-possible for me to accomplish. When I finally began telling her that there were some things I simply couldn't do yet, she was re-ally respectful of my limits. Gradually I started feeling stronger, and even pushed myself, a little at a time. It took a good year for me to function in any kind of manner that resembled the way I used to work."

Find a Balance Between Your Private Grief and Public Self

Tim was the public relations director at a large corporation when his wife, Colette, died. He recalls the lethargy, anxiety, rage, and deep sadness that he felt while on the job and how, eventually, he learned to accept his grief—even on the job:

"When Colette died, I was no longer a husband, I was no longer a lover, and I had lost my friend. Suddenly I was a widower.

"I couldn't cry for five days after my wife's death because I was busy with all the responsibilities and expectations both as a father and as a provider. As a result, my tear ducts got all plugged up and my eyes became infected.

"Returning to work was important to me because my friends were there, but when I returned after two weeks off I realized, to my surprise, that I had no interest in work at all. I had projects to do and I did them, but I worked as little as I could get away with. My work had become almost irrelevant. It no longer held meaning for me.

"For several months, I was either numb or filled with anxiety and uncertainty. I was also exhausted and experienced frequent loss of memory, as if there was some need to forget my work in order to stay in touch with my feelings. It was like degrees of lifting fog, and during the first three weeks on the job I was totally fog-bound.

"I remember once becoming so angry at work that I went into the men's room and punched a metal door. It hurt and I realized how stupid it was to do that. But six months later, when my supervisor confronted me about my drop in productivity, I found that I could finally express my anger toward him in a way that was reasonable and constructive.

"One day I came back from lunch and felt so anxious and tired that I needed to get away from my office. I called a friend and invited myself over to have a cup of coffee with her. She said to me, 'Look, you've always given 120 percent at your job. Now you can coast on 60 percent for a while.' I needed permission to be with my feelings and that was important. I gradually began to cry freely, tell people how I felt, and speak up for myself at work. People would walk by me and look at me crying, and it really didn't make any difference to me. It was wonderful, finally, to know that I could actually be myself in public. I eventually learned that I could say who I was and declare my needs."

WHAT CAN YOU DO?

Seek Permission to Grieve at Work

Oftentimes, managers, bosses, and coworkers show a great deal of compassion and understanding to grieving employees. Recently, for instance, when a newly widowed nurse returned to work after a three-day bereavement leave, her compassionate supervisor assigned a fellow employee to shadow her for the first several weeks. She was encouraged to take time to be by herself and take longer breaks.

Try sitting down with your supervisor and explaining how you feel. Hopefully, together you will be able to negotiate tasks and expectations.

Tell Others About Your Grief Journey

Sometimes losses present opportunities for everyone. Lillian explained it this way:

"I can't tell you how often I heard from people, after only a month and a half after Roy's death, that I should be fine already and get on with my life. 'You have two beautiful girls and a nice house, why are you still upset?' But I was very fortunate to have people at work who were willing to wait for me. You go through life and accumulate stones in your backpack. You always carry them with you. In the beginning you don't know what to do with them or where to put them, but now I know where to put my grief, and how to live beside it. It is still sometimes overwhelming, but now, three years later, I find that it takes less and less time for me to rebound from a really tough day. I remember how my office manager and others at work used to send me little notes to tell me they had faith in me, even when I had none in myself. Those small yet significant gestures, and their willingness to be flexible with job expectations, were invaluable to me. Their willingness to wait for me helped so much."

Work with Your Child to Make a Smooth Transition

Just as coworkers and employers can make all the difference for bereaved adults at work, teachers and schoolmates can be extraordinarily helpful for children returning to school after a loved one dies. Tricia, a fifth grader, believed strongly that school was the place she needed to be after her father's funeral, but she first had to convince her mother to let her go back so soon. When she finally got to class she knew she was right to insist, and that she had found the safe haven she needed.

Tricia's mother was quite taken aback by her daughter's request. "Of course not, honey," she said through her tears. "We'll be taking the limo now to the gravesite where there will be another ceremony and then Daddy will be buried. Then we'll go home and lots of family and friends will meet us there. They'll bring food and spend time with us at our house. I won't go back to work until you tell me you're ready, okay? And you don't have to worry about going to school yet."

Tricia kept insisting until her mother became more confused and angry. "Look," she whispered, "I'm not about to get into a car, at Daddy's funeral, and take you to school. That would be impossible!"

But still Tricia persisted and finally her mother asked her best friend if she would mind driving her. She agreed, and wisely called the school to inform them that Tricia had chosen to come to school directly from her dad's funeral. Tricia arrived at school and walked straight to her classroom. When she opened the door, all of her classmates and her teacher were lined up in a row, waiting for her. One by one, they gave her hugs.

Grieving Doesn't End, Even After You Return to Work or School

Of course, once you're back at work and your child has reintegrated back to school and other activities, your grief continues. Hopefully, with a little assistance, employers, coworkers, fellow students, and school personnel will honor your unfolding journey. The next chapter examines a phenomenon known as magical thinking, a tough, yet predictable aspect of grief for children and adults.

8

Magical Thinking

Magical thinking occurs when a person believes, irrationally, that something he or she said, thought, or wished for was the cause of the death. While certainly common among children, magical thoughts are not exclusive to the very young. Older children, teens, and even adults often grapple with magical thoughts. Whereas in previous chapters I've addressed age groups in five categories (preverbal, two- to five-year-olds, six- to nine-year-olds, ten- to twelve-year-olds, and teens), in this chapter I examine magical thinking within three general categories: younger children, older kids and teens, and adults. First, let's consider younger children up to about nine years of age.

Younger Children's Magical Thoughts

In this age group, children sometimes harbor secret magical thoughts that, if unchecked, can generate prolonged and sometimes damaging self-blame. Children at this age tend to believe that any and all events affecting them or those they love must always be due to their own actions, beliefs, or thoughts. Magical thinking for young children, though irrational and disturbing, is developmentally right on the mark since children at this age tend to lack both the necessary information and maturity required to understand the concept of cause and effect.

You can help your child limit her disturbing magical thoughts by taking these steps:

- First, remember to provide appropriate information about the cause of the death. (This information was discussed in Chapter Four.)
- Next, ask your child why he thinks the death happened. If your child doesn't want to talk about it, then ask him to draw a picture that tells why the death happened and then talk to him about the picture.
- Listen to your child. If he seems to be blaming himself, then you have detected a magical thought.
- Praise your child for being courageous and telling you about it.
- Normalize the magical thought by explaining that lots of people worry that they are responsible when bad things happen.
- Review the information you've already shared with your child about the real cause of death.
- Keep listening to your child's concerns and try to answer any lingering questions.
- Encourage your child to let you know if magical thoughts ever come back, so that you can help him stay on track.

In the next anecdote, Ben was six years old when his brother died of cancer. By taking the steps listed above, I detected and corrected his faulty beliefs about how his brother died.

First, I answered Ben's questions about the cause of his brother's death. Karen Carney's book *What Is Cancer, Anyway?* helped me to explain cancer and cancer treatments to him. It is a young child's coloring book that, in a very simple and concrete fashion, explains the difference between normal cells and cancer cells, what doctors know about cancer, and how it can be treated. (You'll find information on this book and many others in the back of this book.) We also talked about the meaning of death, specifically that his brother's body had completely stopped working and that he would not return to life. A few weeks into our work together, I again asked Ben why he thought his brother died. This sort of question, *if timed properly*, may reveal a magical thought. He replied, "He died because I kicked him in the stomach." Once he revealed this, I addressed the magical thinking directly by praising his courage, since it is never easy to disclose this sort of self-incriminating belief. Then I normalized the concept of magical thinking by explaining to him that most people, even adults, sometimes worry that they have magical powers that make bad things happen. I also did my best to convince Ben that kicking someone or being hurtful toward them never causes cancer. We reviewed Carney's book about cancer and I even invited a pediatric oncology nurse to join one of our sessions to answer some of Ben's more technical questions about cancer. In time, Ben no longer believed that he caused his brother's death.

Sometimes magical thinking persists regardless of how well you implement the above strategy. This was the case with Mary, an eight-year-old whose father died violently in a car accident. Despite her mother's clear explanation about the cause of her father's death, Mary frequently awoke in the middle of the night with a terrifying nightmare that left her convinced she was responsible for her father's death. To address this persistent worry, her mother taught her how to shift from the scary thoughts generated by her recurring nightmare to happier thoughts by making a bead bracelet. The bracelet had five special beads chosen by her daughter to represent five specific, loving memories of her father. A blue bead, for instance, represented the blue terry-cloth bathrobe her father wore as he carried her downstairs to make pancakes every Sunday morning. The bracelet helped Mary focus on specific, positive memories of her father rather than dwelling, as she had been doing, on disturbing and self-blaming magical thoughts.

Older Children and Teens and Magical Thinking

Older children and teens frequently harbor magical thoughts, too, but they are less willing to admit that they have them. When they have magical thoughts it is usually due to having regressed to a younger age. Regression means they are acting in ways normally associated with children who are chronologically younger than they are. Regression in times of crisis is normal, but it can be quite embarrassing for preteens and teens. They are usually sophisticated enough to know that their own magical thoughts are unrealistic, and they may get confused and frustrated if they can't stop their own seemingly childish way of thinking. For this reason, older children and teens tend to suffer silently with their magical thoughts rather than risk admitting to anyone that they have them. They require a modified approach:

- Teach them about the concept of magical thinking, but don't expect them to admit that they are thinking that way.
- Normalize any magical thoughts by explaining that people of all ages, even adults, engage in magical thoughts, especially in crisis.
- Show them specific tools for dealing well with magical thinking, like the bead bracelet method Mary used above. (We'll look at more ideas later in this chapter.)

Adults and Magical Thinking

Magical thoughts are not exclusive to children or teens. You may also have found yourself struggling with them. This was the case with Jordan after her teenage son's death.

Jordan was exasperated by something her son had done and she warned him that if he kept up his foolishness, he wouldn't survive the day. Tragically, he died in a freak accident later that same afternoon. While there was absolutely no logical correlation between Jordan's poorly timed remark and her son's sudden death, for a time she felt strangely responsible because of what she had said to him.

Why would you, or any other intelligent adult, find yourself irrationally blaming yourself for a death? Perhaps, like older children and teens, you've regressed in crisis and are fixated on an irrational way of seeing the world. If this is the case, you can learn strategies to deal with these feelings.

Why We Blame Ourselves

While magical thinking is a misguided form of self-blame, it may also protect you from the frightening notion that no matter how hard you try to control what happens in your family, random events still occur. Without yourself to blame, you might conclude that terrible things sometimes simply happen for no rhyme or reason, and that everything seems random and futile. Like many parents, Julia believed that no matter what, no matter the circumstances, parents are always responsible for keeping their children safe. Her belief became unbearably difficult when her infant died in her arms at home with absolutely no warning. She raced to the ER, where her baby was declared dead on arrival.

For weeks afterward, Julia insisted that she was entirely to blame for her daughter's death, despite assurances to the contrary from the medical team at the hospital.

After her daughter's death, there was no one to blame but herself. Nothing anyone said would convince her otherwise. One doctor who had only just met her told her she was a very good mother and should stop feeling guilty. A friend insisted that she needed to stop blaming herself or she would lose her mind. All of their efforts failed to eliminate Julia's persistent magical belief that she was to blame for her child's death. At last, when the autopsy results arrived, her child's doctor explained how a very rare illness killed her daughter, and that due to the rapid onset of symptoms, it would even have gone undetected if her baby had been admitted to the pediatric ICU before showing any symptoms whatsoever. In effect, not even the best medical minds could have saved her child. Julia was finally satisfied that she was not responsible, but this only caused her more distress. If random tragedies like her daughter's death could happen, she thought, then no parent can completely ensure the safety of his or her child. Unable now to blame even herself, she was filled with anxiety about the countless ways her children could be at risk.

Disengaging from your magical thoughts won't necessarily relieve you of all your distress, and, as Julia came to realize, self-blame can sometimes seem the lesser of two painful ways of viewing your world. For this reason, before dismissing your magical thoughts, ask yourself these questions:

- If there were a spiritual lesson that came with your magical thinking, what might it be?
- What would it take to acknowledge your own limitations and possibly forgive yourself?
- Can you forgive others who you have been holding responsible for your loss?

- Has your faith been shaken by your loss? How?
- Could you ever forgive your God for allowing this death to have happened?

Once you explore magical thoughts by asking yourself these questions, there is a better chance that you'll leave them behind someday, and move forward with your grief.

Eventually, if you desire to move on from magical thinking but find that you feel stuck, try attending to some of your own feelings of culpability by remembering that:

- Magical thinking is normal, even for adults.
- Magical thinking for adults is one way of attempting to make terrible things seem avoidable. In other words, if you were truly at fault, then you could learn to be more responsible and prevent further deaths from happening in your family.
- If you're inclined to be reflective about your magical thoughts, you may want to ask yourself how magical thinking might be providing a sense of order in your world that you need right now. You may also want to consider what it would take to forgive yourself, if, in fact, you were somehow responsible for some of the events that have transpired.
- If you believe you are ready to let go of your magical thoughts, then consider taking some of the measures below to mitigate them.

WHAT YOU CAN DO

For younger children, a well-timed inquiry like "Why do you think it happened?" may reveal a magical thought. Then, once revealed, you can take up the conversation by:

- Praising your child's courage.
- Normalizing magical thinking by explaining to your child that people of all ages often find themselves thinking this way.
- Patiently correcting your child's error in thinking. You can use books that teach about the cause of various illnesses. The list of books in the Resources section can assist you in your exploration. You can also call on experts with medical expertise to help you or your child understand.

Older children and teens are likely to feel too embarrassed by their magical thoughts to reveal them. For them, simply explain the concept of magical thinking and offer concrete suggestions. The following five suggestions can help them let go of their belief that they have somehow caused the death.

1. *Reality testing*: Explain that when a magical thought persists, it helps to gently remind yourself that while magical thinking is a very normal phenomenon, it is illogical and can always be corrected. For instance, challenge a magical thought by remembering that some people believe cancer is contagious, but doctors know that it is not.

2. *Magic stone*: While going for a walk with your child, suggest looking for a special stone that feels good to hold and fits easily in her pocket. This stone can become a sort of talisman to remind her of those things she values most in the world. Then, if a magical thought persists, she can hold the stone in her hand. It will help her focus on more positive thoughts.

3. *Affirmation scroll*: Make a scroll out of parchment or any special paper, and inscribe on it all the positive things that you attribute to your child. Be honest. Be generous. This scroll can become an important resource when magical thoughts

get the best of her and she needs to be reminded of her strengths and skills.

4. *Memory bracelet*: Go to a bead store with your child and ask her to choose five beads that represent five cherished memories about the person who died. Make a bracelet together. During difficult times, the beads can help your child shift away from painful magical thoughts.

5. *Thought-stopping flash card*: Make a set of flash cards with your child. On one side draw a stop sign. On the other, write an affirmation statement or description of a brief pleasant memory of your child's choosing. If a magical thought persists, your child can get out her cards, look at the stop sign, and then read the positive words on the other side of the card.

Magical thinking is normal at any age. By following the suggestions in this chapter you can help your child or teen stop needless self-blame. Remember that you also may have become caught up in your own magical thoughts. This is normal. Sometimes the same corrective steps described in this chapter for your child can be useful for you. You can tweak any of the strategies to fit your needs. Other times, however, magical thoughts are there to help you in your struggle to understand the magnitude of your loss, in which case, rather than dismissing them outright, you may wish to examine them more closely, either on your own or with a professional, and learn from them.

WHAT TO REMEMBER

Now that you've begun to face the terrible news of a death and you're learning ways to manage initial reactions like denial, anxiety, and numbness, you hopefully are also discovering that you can still effectively parent your child. You've also learned effective strategies for explaining to your child what has happened and you have learned how to mentor your child on his grief journey. You understand now what makes childhood grief unique at particular stages of their lives and how to meet your child's needs as he grows up. In addition, you've been introduced to ways of integrating young people into funerals and other death rituals, and how, as you return to work, you can assist your youngster in returning to school. Finally, you've learned how to help your child manage magical thoughts, and you've begun to appreciate how your own magical thoughts can be a catalyst for better understanding the many faces of your own grief.

Part Three will address the next phase of grieving, the second storm. Try to remember that grief is not as linear as the words we use to describe it. The ideas, issues, and concerns you've faced so far don't stop when the second storm of grief arrives. Grief reactions keep recycling over time, so you'll want to refer back to this section of the book again and again as your journey unfolds.

PART THREE

THE SECOND STORM

9

Entering the Second Phase of Grief

Living well while grieving often requires coming to the realization that the journey will be long and hard, and that it won't follow a simple healing path. The second phase of grief, called the second storm, may take your breath away because it feels sudden and unexpected, so as you read on, be sure to take time to sit still and slowly breath in and out.

The Second Storm Is Often Unexpected

I learned about the second storm of grief just after my father died. I received many caring words of condolence from friends and family, but perhaps the most helpful remark came from Edith, one of my dad's closest friends. After the funeral, she was brief, direct, caring, and honest. "Rob," she told me, "you'll never *really* get over this." It has been over thirty-five years since my dad's death, and I continue to be grateful to Edith for her wise counsel. She let me in on one of life's best-kept secrets, that our greatest losses may change us forever. Unfortunately, this reality isn't talked about enough.

You need to be aware that grief is tough and erratic, especially during the second storm. You will have good days and very difficult days. The second storm comes suddenly, unexpectedly. While it is normal and predictable, many will think it means that you're grieving out of order, as if all your grief should have occurred on an even-keeled trajectory. They are wrong. In the following anecdote, Jim, a patient of mine, told me how his pain during the second storm was not at all what his colleagues expected, which left him feeling lonelier than ever.

Five months after his daughter's death, Jim realized that when his coworkers asked how he was doing, they were really expecting him to tell them that he was feeling better. But in fact, he felt overwhelmed with despair, his life felt meaningless, and he frequently could not control his crying jags. When he told his coworkers the truth, they'd shake their heads and walk away, leaving him feeling vulnerable, desperately lonely, and even more isolated than before. So Jim started telling people what they wanted to hear. "Things are getting better," he told them. "I'm feeling a little less pain every day and I can really see the light at the end of the tunnel." But lying to them only made him feel lonelier.

Jim was coming to terms with something many grievers have shared with me over the years, and that is that very few people seem to understand grief as a complicated trajectory of feelings and reactions that don't typically resolve in days, weeks, or even months. The second storm is a time when grief comes back at you, perhaps harder than ever before, usually when you're already back at work and your child has returned to school, and just when family, friends, coworkers, and employers are expecting you to start feeling better rather than worse.

Common Feelings in the Second Storm

There is no single prescription for grief. Too often, the bereaved start thinking that to grieve correctly means fulfilling some expert's expectations. While there is a broad range of emotional reactions during the second storm, you don't need to follow any particular order of feelings and you needn't be concerned about having to express every feeling mentioned below. There are, however, some feelings and reactions that many grievers experience during the second storm. They include:

- *Anger:* There is, after all, so much to be angry about. While perfectly normal, anger may seem irrational or inappropriate to you. For instance, you may be angry with the deceased for abandoning you; or angry with yourself for not being a perfect partner, friend, parent, son, or daughter; or angry at God or at the randomness of events that have occurred. You may even rage in ways that startle you. This is all normal.
- *Fear and panic:* The extraordinary changes that come with your loss may be terribly frightening.
- *Guilt and self-blame:* Deep regret for things said or unsaid, things done or not done, are often a part of the grief process.
- *Profound sadness:* Things that are truly hurtful often generate overwhelming emptiness.
- *Lost sense of self:* You may start questioning the meaning of your very existence. Along with loss of meaning and purpose you may even sometimes wish to die.
- *Physical illness:* Not only is grief usually exhausting, but it also places your nervous system and immune system under extreme stress. Common grief reactions include: dizziness, dry mouth, tightness in the throat, rashes, tension headaches,

fatigue, insomnia, sighing, pronounced startle response, aching muscles, lingering colds, recurring flu, and nausea.

While these are all normal reactions, sometimes they persist and start to interfere with your ability to function effectively in the world. Part Five will look at signs of problematic grief, but in this chapter we will look at what some would call "the dark night of the soul." Many bereaved people find solace in reaching out to family, friends, clergy, and/or support groups and bereavement professionals, while others find greater benefit in establishing a more solitary time for reflection. Both approaches are okay, and regardless of whether you grieve collaboratively or not, I urge you to create a safe haven for yourself to support your journey.

Create a Safe Haven for Yourself

A safe haven is your personal sanctuary. It can be anywhere you choose: in your home, in a counseling office, in a grief support group, with a friend or by yourself, in a religious sanctuary, in a quiet clearing in the woods or a busy cafe. Once in your safe place, consider doing three things:

1. *Identify what you are feeling or thinking about:* For instance, you may be unbearably sad as you long for the person who has died; furious at yourself, someone else, or at God; guilty about something you said or didn't say; hurt by someone's thoughtlessness; frightened by the emptiness you feel; confused by feelings of relief, exhaustion, or your inability to even get out of bed; surprised by your interest in sex at a time like this; or struck by the absolute meaninglessness of your life.

2. *Express yourself*: There are endless possibilities for self-expression. For instance, you can talk it out with a friend or counselor, journal, paint or draw, chop wood, run, play music, garden, walk your dog, meditate, pray, or howl at the moon.

3. *Share your safe place*: Consider inviting someone you trust into your safe place. Remember, though, that while sharing with someone who cares can be extraordinarily therapeutic, it is also okay to keep your safe haven as private as you want it to be.

Identifying, expressing, and sharing won't take your grief away, but it will help you to gently move forward on your journey. For instance, once you safely express some anger, you'll probably identify a different feeling or thought to express and perhaps share next. While the safe haven won't take away the pain, it will keep your grief dynamic. At this point in the process, your grief journey is really about shifting and changing reactions or feelings. Rather than being stuck in one single feeling or reaction, the best thing you can do for yourself is to create opportunities to express the rich range of feelings that encompass your journey.

Write Down Your Feelings

Many grievers have found solace in journaling. It can be a great way to identify, express, and perhaps share what you've been feeling, thinking, and doing on your grief journey. I suggest you get a notebook or pad and pen, and set aside a particular time of the day when you have some privacy and are not likely to be distracted. Sometimes journaling is enhanced with a writing prompt. Examples of prompts are inspirational poems, evocative songs, or meaningful photographs that gently direct your thoughts and feelings. Or by simply sitting quietly, the silence itself often becomes a prompt. Throughout this book I'll suggest various writing prompts that you may find useful.

A Writing Prompt

Reflect on your grief as an unfolding process of discovery. Ask yourself: How have I been grieving lately?

While you may choose to keep your journal entry entirely private, you may want to share your writing with a family member or friend, maybe even with someone close to you who seems to be pushing you to end your grief prematurely.

As you continue reading Part Three, you'll explore more dimensions of the second storm. The next chapter examines how grief is expressed in a broad range of normal and healthy ways, and how families can learn to embrace their differences by listening deeply to one another.

10

Debunking Common
Misunderstandings About Grief

Elizabeth Kübler-Ross's book *On Death and Dying,* published in 1969, tore down many strict taboos the medical community had against any kind of forthright conversation with the terminally ill about what they were experiencing and any real discussion about death and dying. Rather than avoiding the topic of death and grief, Kübler-Ross was the first physician to face the subject head-on, and, in doing so, she empowered people everywhere who were approaching death to become teachers themselves on the subject of grief and loss. Her book caught the public's attention, ushered in the American hospice movement, and started a national conversation about matters of life and death that continues to this day. Kübler-Ross identified five stages of dying that emerged from her conversations with dying patients: denial, anger, bargaining, depression, and acceptance. While these stages were never intended to establish any strict rule of order for the bereaved, they have entered the popular culture and, unfortunately, sometimes plague grievers with unnecessary expectations that are placed upon them, suggesting there is only one correct pathway to grieve.

For instance, a minister attending one of my seminars told me that he had to be grieving incorrectly because he hadn't felt any anger since his brother's death. I suggested that he try trusting his own process by allowing his feelings to unfold naturally. That way, if he were ever to feel anger toward his brother for dying, he'd know it came from him and not from someone else's rulebook.

This chapter is an attempt to debunk two common misunderstandings about grief: that everyone's grief looks the same, and that grief always makes you feel helpless.

The 1st Misunderstanding: Everyone's Grief Should Look Alike

Getting Over It, Filling the Emptiness, and Keeping the Connection

Three styles of grieving were identified by researcher Ida Martinson, who studied a group of bereaved parents over the course of seven years. The study, called "The Empty Space Phenomenon," can be found in Ken Doka's book *Children Mourning, Mourning Children*, cited in the Resources. Her findings help clarify, for grievers of all sorts of losses, that there is no single way to grieve. Do any of the following three styles capture the way you've been grieving?

Getting Over It: You don't look back or dwell on the past. Perhaps you haven't completely gotten over your loss, but you're learning to place your grief in a very safe place where it no longer interferes with the way you lead your life.

Filling the Emptiness: You try to keep busy in all sorts of ways in order to reduce or even eliminate the painful feelings that come with your loss. For instance, you may have joined a support group, or taken on a leadership role in a support group you've been attending, or perhaps you have immersed yourself in your job and found great meaning that way, or you might be committed to honoring your loved one's memory through acts of kindness or service. Other examples of filling the emptiness include remarrying, moving into a new home, or deciding to have more children. Regardless of how you choose to fill the void, you've found yourself able to reduce the ache of your grief, except during brief surges of pain on anniversaries of the death or during other triggering times in your life.

Keeping the Connection: You consider the pain of grief to be an important link to your loved one, so you embrace it. It may be interesting to note that the participants in the study who kept the connection reported that gradually the pain diminished by itself, freeing them up to expand their lives beyond the narrow confines of their losses.

Whether you get over it, fill up the emptiness, keep the connection, or grieve in some other way entirely, I encourage you to embrace how you grieve. The Martinson study provides a useful framework for identifying your own approach to grieving. If any of these three ways rings true for you, remember that they are all valid grief reactions. However, each approach presents potential problems, too. For instance, by focusing on getting over it you may be delaying or avoiding some of your grief work. Sometimes people fill the emptiness with alcohol or other unhealthy substances, which, of course, would be problematic. Keeping the connection can sometimes become immobilizing and self-limiting. Any of these challenges would indicate a form of problematic grieving, which we'll address in Chapter Seventeen.

A Closer Look at "Keeping the Connection"

There often isn't room in our fast-paced, productivity-oriented society for grief and mourning. Instead, there is a lot of talk about "recovery" and "closure," as if grieving were something to skip over on the way to healing. Therefore, if you tend to establish strong links to memories of your loved one, your style may be frowned upon by those who emphasize the benefits of getting over it as soon as possible. If members of your family or any friends challenge this style, here are some questions to ask yourself that may help you determine whether or not keeping the connection is working for you:

- Is there room in your heart for different styles to live together in peace within your family? Hopefully you are able to allow others in your family to find their own way, even if they tend not to hold on as you do.
- Is your way of holding on harmful to yourself or to others? Hopefully, this is not the case and you are discovering effective ways to balance a whole range of feelings as you stay connected to your memories.
- Do you think your approach to holding on is taking over your life or limiting your effectiveness in the world? For a time, grieving usually puts life as we once knew it on hold, so perhaps you don't know yet whether or not your way of grieving will ultimately support a process of healing for you. This will become clearer to you over time.

The Franklin family tended to hold on by keeping connected to their loved one who had died. Their family doctor was alarmed to learn that for ten years after their son's death, they kept their son's bedroom intact, just as it had been before his death. All of his clothing, books, toys, and stuffed animals remained in the room. To the doctor, this all seemed quite morbid and unhealthy, but they wanted to determine for themselves whether or not their home-based shrine was contributing to any significant family dysfunction.

By asking the above questions, they discovered that they all approved of keeping the room as is, and that they had no rigid rules and regulations about how to behave in the bedroom or how frequently to go inside the room. Once in the room, they usually prayed, meditated, or reminisced, and when they left the room, they felt peaceful and uplifted. In general, they were a high-functioning family whose lives weren't limited by keeping a shrine. On the contrary, it seemed that their decision to maintain the child's bedroom as it had been while he was alive contributed to their mental health by helping them to embrace their shared loss while learning to move forward with their lives.

What to Do When Others Try to Shut Down Your Grief

Like the Franklin family, you may also face disapproval and judgment from others. Too often grief is minimized, reduced, and sanitized by family, friends, and coworkers. It seems, sometimes, that there is no safe place to grieve openly. In the face of persistent disapproval, sometimes we shut down and start keeping grief secrets.

If your grief has begun to feel like "the elephant in the living room" that nobody wants to acknowledge anymore, you may have taken your grieving underground to avoid the constant judgment of those around you. For instance, you may have begun telling others that you've moved on, when in fact you've been suffering in silence. Instead of going underground like that, I urge you to keep on trying to find someone worthy of your trust. My grand-mother is an example of someone who seemed to have no one to turn to after her daughter's death, which caused her much needless suffering.

Grandma was a great storyteller who loved to share poignant memories of a simpler childhood in the Ukraine, and vivid de-scriptions of loved ones who died in the Holocaust, but she also harbored a secret grief that was the result of a strict family rule not to talk about her child that had died. For most of my child-hood, Grandma lived like a hermit in our house. She cooked her own simple meals and ate by herself in her small studio bedroom upstairs. She hardly ever joined us at the dinner table. On holi-days, my parents tried to coax her down for a family meal, and on the rare occasions when she joined us, she stood awkwardly, plate in hand, alongside our dining room table. She never sat on any of our chairs or couches, afraid she would wear out our furniture. When not alone in her bedroom, she would sit on the landing at the top of the front stairs, wringing her hands and imagining every possible disaster that could befall each member of our household. I never realized how strange these behaviors were until I was older and started comparing her to my friends' grandparents.

I was about twelve years old when I first joined Grandma, Uncle Joe, Aunt Rhoda, and my four cousins on their annual pil-grimage to my grandfather's New Jersey gravesite. The vast ceme-tery was like an ancient city, and my uncle maneuvered the narrow roads with ease and parked the car under a gnarled pine tree. They all had a job to do. My aunt and uncle carried out the plant clippers, rakes, shovels, and other gardening tools. My cousins unloaded all of the assorted perennials and annuals from the trunk. Grandma got out of the car and walked right past Grandpa's grave to the other side of a grove of trees. Her knees caved and she started to wail and moan and shake. My relatives kept busy with their chores, weeding and planting around Grandpa's gravesite, ignoring Grandma, who sank to the ground holding tightly to a very small gravestone. I stepped closer to her and saw the name *Pauline* inscribed on the stone. When they finished gardening, all of us, except Grandma, walked quietly back to the car and piled inside. Then, through the cloudy car window, I watched my uncle Joe walk back to Grandma, bend down, carry her frail, limp body back to the car, and squeeze her into the backseat beside me.

Of course I wanted to find out more about Pauline, but to my great surprise, neither my father nor anyone else in the family would answer my questions about her, and I was told to never mention her name again. Many years later, after my grandmother and my father had died, I worked up the courage to ask my uncle about Pauline. She died of polio at the age of ten, and my grandmother seemed so distressed after her daughter's death that the whole family became frightened for her and insisted that everyone, including her, stop talking about Pauline and move on with their lives. The family rule lasted for over fifty years. While going through her things after she died, I found a framed photograph of a young girl in my grandmother's bureau drawer. Maybe when she was alone, she took it out and wept. Or maybe she only cried once a year at her daughter's grave.

Deeply held secrets, like my grandmother's, sometimes shape lives. Many of her coping strategies—her refusal to join our family at mealtimes, fearing that she'd wear out her welcome by sitting on our furniture, worrying obsessively about us—seemed to stem from the long-standing family rule that everyone must act as if Pauline never existed. Paradoxically, my grandmother and other members of my family still *held on* to Pauline's memory, albeit in a problematic way, by attempting to bury her memory along with her body. I wish that my grandmother knew that there were people who would have listened to her and honored her story. If, like my grandmother, you feel compelled to act as if your grief has ended, but you still harbor deep feelings of mourning, you are not alone. Find someone among your family and friends whom you trust, or consider attending a grief support group. "Finding a Grief Support Center" (page 194) can also direct you to grief support resources near where you live.

Grief does not look or feel the same for everyone. Your way of grieving is the result of a combination of factors that include your personality, family rituals, religious practice, ethnic traditions, cultural rules, and even regional norms. Everyone's grief process is a journey of discovery that has its own unique twists and turns. For this reason, when I work with the bereaved, I'll often say, "Teach me how you grieve." Then, as their personal style of grief emerges, the work at hand becomes clearer.

Questions to Help You Find Your Style of Grieving

- Do you tend to be emotionally expressive or more stoic? Do ethnic and religious traditions influence how you and others in your family grieve? How?
- Have cultural or religious expectations been a burden or a blessing to you and others in your family? For instance, do you feel at ease with how you are expected to grieve, or have you felt out of sync with cultural and religious beliefs and practices?
- How differently do men and women in your family tend to mourn? What have you learned from your parents about this?
- Since in most families there are unspoken rules about how to express grief, have you broken any of your family's rules

since your loss? If so, how comfortable are you forging your own path? Have there been disagreements or disputes among family members or within your community concerning how you should grieve?

Once you've considered these questions you'll better understand your particular approach to grief.

Not All Grief Is Expressed Through Feelings

Do you express your grief physically more than emotionally? Are you more likely to think about your loss then express feelings of grief? Have you been reading about grief, but notice that you're not crying as much as those around you? Have you become actively engaged in grief-related activities such as building a casket, designing a memorial quilt, or planning a memorial service? Does your loss sometimes seem like a problem that you've been trying your best to solve? Rather than talking about feelings, are you more comfortable chopping wood, engaging in sports, or even having sex? When friends ask you how you feel, are you at a loss?

If you answered in the affirmative to any of these questions, your way of grieving may seem strange or inappropriate to those who think good grieving must be a feeling-focused process. It really doesn't have to be, and your grief is just as valid as that of an emotionally laden griever, you just express it differently. To better understand this, let's look at how grief styles are influenced by gender expectations. If you were to take a poll among your friends and family, you'd probably find that women tend to be more feeling-focused then men. This may have to do with the cultural expectation that men are supposed to be stoic and in charge of things, and women are expected to be emotional and needy. In truth, grief styles are not determined by gender, and there are many feeling-focused men and action-oriented women. Nevertheless, we still hear it said that men don't cry and, therefore, don't grieve. A group of married couples I worked with provide a good example of how helpful it can be to look beyond the limitations of gender-defined expectations.

In a couples group for bereaved parents, the men all worked outside the home and the women stayed home to raise the children. At first their ways of grieving seemed pretty standard: The women cried and the men sat awkwardly in silence. On the surface, the men seemed to function perfectly well outside the group. Each morning they left behind whatever minimal grief they felt and went off to work. The "real" grievers were the women, who stayed home all day, absorbed in grief. The subject of gender came up in the group when several women revealed how unfair their lives seemed and how they resented their husbands for being so insensitive and unloving, as evidenced by how easy it seemed for them to leave for work each morning. Fortunately this led to a heated discussion that eventually revealed some deeper truths. Several men revealed how painful it was for them to leave the house each morning, and that they wished they could linger at home and be available to support their wives. Then the women admitted that they'd been harboring a desire to leave and get some relief from their stifling and depressing houses. As gender stereotypes broke down, they were able to renegotiate their roles to meet actual needs and desires rather than societal expectations. They also began to better understand that both going out to work and staying at home were valid expressions of caring and love within grieving families.

Just as couples have unique ways of grieving due to various gender expectations, some differences may also be due to factors that stem from differences in personality, beliefs, and psychological makeup. I spoke with a young minister who was struck by two starkly different bereavement styles at the funeral of an infant.

Pastor John was fresh out of seminary and recently installed in his first parish. His first funeral was for a baby who died from sudden infant death syndrome (SIDS). Pastor John, who had an infant of his own, found himself feeling quite emotional as he performed his duties. At the graveside service, he observed friends and family holding up the devastated mother. During a break in the service, a concerned neighbor of the family took him aside and pointed to the baby's father, who was standing alone, stone-faced, and clutching a finely handcrafted wooden cradle. "He was working on that cradle the night his baby died," the neighbor told Pastor John. "He's been in his workshop finishing that cradle ever since, so that it would be done in time for the funeral, I guess." After the mourners had all left, Pastor John, haunted by the father's unusual behavior and by how isolated he seemed at his own child's funeral, sat alone in his car and wept for that couple and for their child.

He had witnessed what may have been a breakdown in communication between a grieving couple. Later the pastor wondered if the father's apparent stoicism was due to his lack of ability to grieve, or whether he was, in his own way, actively grieving his child's death. After reflecting further, Pastor John concluded that the man may have been a deeply devoted father merely demonstrating his own type of grief. He wondered, though, whether the wife was confused and hurt by her husband's lack of expression of feelings at the burial, which may have seemed cold and uncaring to her. Pastor John also wondered if the father felt ignored by his family and friends, who surrounded his wife and left him standing alone at the graveside.

Practice Deep Listening

Family members often encounter extreme variations in their grief styles, and as a result have serious misunderstandings. Learning to listen carefully to one another will help you avoid an unnecessary breakdown in communication in your family. Due to different approaches to grief, deep listening is an effective way for family members in conflict to make peace and solve their problems. Deep listening has four steps:

1. Remember that even if family members disagree with or feel hurt by the actions or style of others in the family, no one person in the family is responsible for fixing this problem.
2. Remember that neither you nor anyone else in your family is obligated to fundamentally change how you grieve.
3. Try teaching one another, as plainly as possible, what it is that you need to happen.
4. Agree to take turns reflecting back to one another exactly what you heard the other person say they need.

When family members with conflicting styles of grieving don't listen well enough, relationships can deteriorate. In the following anecdote, Tom and his teenage daughters' differences generated a hurtful argument that led to an impasse.

Like many widows and widowers, Tom felt a strong desire to mark the first anniversary of his wife's birthday with a family ritual. Anniversary dates, such as birthdays and dates of deaths, are often laden with memories and have great significance for family members. After much consideration, Tom decided to stay home from work for the day, and his plan involved asking his two daughters to join him. They'd light a birthday candle in his wife's memory, and then gather around the dining room table to look at family photo albums together and reminisce. They'd cook a special meal together and then, after dinner, go to the cemetery to lay a wreath. Although the plan felt rich and meaningful to him, his daughters refused to participate. Instead, they insisted on staying in school on their mother's birthday in order to keep things as normal as possible. Tom felt abandoned, hurt, and furious at his daughters. He demanded that they stay home from school and join his ritual, and when they refused, called them ungrateful and unfeeling. They called him morbid and said his plan was stupid.

Tom was not wrong for wanting to mark his wife's birthday with a ritual that would involve his daughters, and the girls weren't wrong for disliking their father's plan, but their different styles churned up an unproductive and hurtful argument. When they learned to practice deep listening they were able to get beyond their differences and resolve the impasse.

Tom began by calmly explaining to them that rituals were always special to their mother and that he had thought long and hard about honoring her birthday as a family. Then the girls told Tom that their mother's birthday would be tough for them, too, but being stuck at home all day was the last thing they needed. At school, they explained, they'd have their friends to support them. Then Tom and the girls sat together in silence and, after a few moments, the girls asked for some time to confer together in the next room. When they returned, they told their father that they would take the morning off from school to participate in a ritual at home with him, but then they'd return to school in time for lunch. Their compromise helped solve a family problem that had seemed insurmountable.

Couples can also benefit from listening deeply. I helped a

bereaved couple that was deeply conflicted come to a peaceful resolution.

I met Helen and Chuck a few weeks before Christmas, only six months after their five-year-old, Sarah, died in a drowning accident. The holidays were approaching, and Chuck looked forward to hanging Sarah's favorite Christmas ornament on their tree. Helen, on the other hand, was enraged at him for being so insensitive, because having the decoration in plain sight would be traumatizing for her. At our first meeting, Chuck accused Helen of being hurtful and inconsiderate, and Helen called Chuck callous and manipulative.

I asked them to release one another from all obligations to fix their feelings; avoid any expectations that either of them must change; try to explain to each other, as plainly as possible, what they needed; and take turns repeating what they heard the other say.

Chuck told Helen that the angel represented Sarah's sweet spirit and that by hanging it up on their tree he'd find some peace during an otherwise intolerable holiday season. And then Helen told Chuck that she knew this Christmas would be filled with many unbearable triggers, and she would need to be extremely careful in order to survive, too. She told him how frightened she was when she anticipated seeing their daughter's angel on the tree. Chuck assured Helen that he understood how much pain she'd feel if she were forced to see the angel on their tree each day. As I had hoped would happen, the tone of their conversation had shifted from adversarial to respectful, loving, and even collaborative. I then instructed them to sit together in silence for a moment. Finally, Chuck turned to Helen and said, "I'd like to take the angel to work and hang it on the tree in my office." At last, they had discovered a compromise.

There is no guarantee that deep listening will result in a peaceful solution to your family's issues, but your chances of success will improve when you drop your defenses, stop fighting, and start listening respectfully to each other. Of course, this is not easy to do, because grief makes you feel raw and needy. It takes all the strength you can muster to break through your own wishes for the grieving process and place your faith in its natural progression. Deep listening is really about believing that your family can deal with your differences and being willing to respect one another even while you're hurting.

The 2nd Misunderstanding: You Will Always Feel Helpless as You Grieve

It is normal to feel overwhelmed. But for a day or perhaps a particular moment in a day, you will also notice that you have found your stride again. Cherish those precious times when you discover your strength, even as you acknowledge feeling helpless.

Feeling Helpless Is Normal

Feeling helpless often comes with grief. After all, your loss has taken your breath away, and the intensity of early grief has left you unable to fully grasp what has happened to you and your family. In addition, your anxiety has reached a crescendo you've never felt before, and you have found that in order to survive you need to lean on family, friends, and perhaps even strangers for support. This is all normal grief and yet it can be crazy making. Feeling helpless comes with the territory.

Difficult Feelings Will Come and Go

You may have already noticed that there have been moments, hours, perhaps even days, when you have surprised yourself with an uncanny ability to suddenly be able to function well in the midst of the roller coaster of your grief. Perhaps you've been able to organize a family photo album, or pay some of your bills, or go food shopping, or read a story to your child, or attend a parent-teacher meeting at your child's school. Afterward you may have felt exhausted and slipped back into the overwhelming morass of your grief once again. This, too, is normal. I don't know for sure why this occurs, but I suspect that it might be your body's way of pacing the grief process. As we struggle to get through the tough times, it is easy to miss the progress we've made. In the following story, Joan was so concerned by the intensity of her feelings after her husband's death that she failed to notice the strides she had been making on her journey.

Joan had been married for thirty-five years. Her husband's death from cancer was sudden and senseless and, at first, life without him felt intolerable. Early on, she worried that her grief had gotten out of control. When alone at home she screamed at the walls and kicked the furniture. It was helpful for her to learn that normal grieving often gets crazy and extreme like that. Joan was what I call a "type A," a person who always strove to grieve perfectly. She took notes during all our sessions and left each meeting with a to-do list that clarified her goals and objectives for the week. One objective was to start working out again at the YMCA. Exercise was important to her, but she had been avoiding going to the gym because it triggered memories of times she and her husband had taken exercise classes together. Such triggers are common after a loss, and they often subside over time, so

I suggested that she slowly ease back into an exercise regime, perhaps starting by walking around her neighborhood with a friend. One morning, Joan rushed into my office several minutes late for our session. She apologized, explaining that she had been to the gym and somehow had miscalculated the time. I pointed out that I was glad to hear that she'd achieved one of her goals. She paused a moment, smiled, and said, "I guess I am getting a little stronger."

Sometimes Your Own Resilience Will Surprise You

Like Joan, you, too, will sometimes surprise yourself with evidence of renewed strength. Try becoming aware of the little things you've accomplished, like finding the courage to reach out to a friend for support, or getting out to the grocery store by yourself, or even laughing at a joke for the first time. Small steps like these are indicators of emerging shifts in your bereavement process. They are signs of your inner strength even in the midst of helplessness, and of your innate ability to pace yourself as you grieve.

There are many ways to grieve. We've just examined a few. You may identify with a combination of styles in this chapter, or you may have found your grief to be entirely different. Honor your grief, and remember that conflicts in families sometimes arise out of differences. If this is happening in your family, try to listen deeply to one another. Remember, too, that your grief will probably include periods of helplessness with unexpected moments of coping, so be patient and celebrate your resilience whenever you're able.

Writing Prompts

Consider whether or not you have been harboring any grief secrets. If so, have a conversation with your secret grief. You might start by writing "I am grateful to you for . . ." or "You have made my grieving more difficult because . . ." Ask yourself when it might be appropriate to reveal a grief secret to someone you trust.

If you've been feeling helpless as you grieve, try to write about any other times in your past when you suffered great adversity and found the strength you needed to survive. Ask yourself how you can draw upon that strength right now.

WHAT TO REMEMBER

There will be differences and, most likely, times of conflict in your family. When this occurs, practice deep listening.

- First, remember that when you disagree or feel hurt by another's actions or style, no one individual is responsible for fixing the problem.
- Second, don't expect yourself or anyone else in the family to change.
- Third, try teaching one another what you need.
- Fourth, take turns reflecting back what you heard the other person say to you.
- Then wait. Perhaps you and your loved ones will start seeing things a little differently, and your conflict will begin to resolve.

How to Help Your Child Manage Big Feelings

Your child's grief is unique, but you can help him manage a range of grief reactions. Don't forget that children grieve, even though their behavior may sometimes suggest otherwise. Let's take another look at childhood grief by age to consider how childhood developmental stages affect how young people respond to loss.

Your Preverbal Child

Very young children are unable to grasp the basic facts of death and can't yet express themselves in words. It would be easy, then, to assume that your very young child will not grieve, but this is not true. First, he must experience what he has lost over time, and eventually he will feel the absence of the person who has died. Once he feels his loss, he will struggle to express his grief, often through repetitive physical activity, such as kicking or throwing objects, or crying out. You can help by bearing witness to how he expresses himself. Use your own words to describe what you see, such as: "I see how hard you threw your ball. You look very angry!" Paying attention to your child this way may not stop him from feeling pain, but your observations and comments, along with holding and nurturing, will let your child know you are there with him and that you care.

Your Two- to Five-Year-Old

Crying isn't the only way to express sadness and grief. At this age children try very hard to grasp the meaning of death. Your child probably keeps forgetting that the dead body has stopped working, and that his loved one will never return. As he struggles to make sense of his loss, physical activity, such as spontaneous movement or song or other forms of play, may be his only way of releasing painful feelings. While your child's laughter or desire to play may suggest to you that he isn't grieving or doesn't care, these are age-appropriate ways of releasing feelings and/or establishing normalcy and control during difficult times. What appears to be indifference is really your child's attempt to grapple with a painful loss. What your child needs most from you is your guidance and understanding. Often the best thing you can do is to remain loving, and remember to patiently repeat your explanations of death as needed.

A personal anecdote from my own childhood illustrates the kind of behavior a young child may exhibit when confronted with death. I was five years old when my best friend's mother died. While my reactions reflected a range of grief responses, on the surface, I probably appeared to be doing anything but grieving.

Michael was my buddy and next-door neighbor when his mom was killed in a car accident. This was my first encounter with the death of someone close to me. That same day, my friend Kim and

I stood in my driveway bordering Michael's front yard and chanted over and over, "Michael Johnson's mother is dead! Michael Johnson's mother is dead!" We got louder and louder and sillier and sillier as we giggled and jumped to the rhythm of our song. Suddenly we became very self-conscious and stopped. Kim and I never talked about this incident, but for years, whenever I remembered our strange game, I felt deeply embarrassed. I used to hope that nobody saw us or heard us there on the driveway, because we must have looked and sounded like very bad children making a poor joke about a terrible tragedy.

You may wonder why Kim and I exhibited such strange and seemingly inappropriate behavior. I imagine that we felt terribly frightened by a sudden death that probably seemed more real to us than we'd ever imagined death could be. If our friend Michael's mother could die, then our parents could also die. This was unthinkable. Our repetitive play and laughter was probably our way of deflecting a very frightening situation and releasing our fears and worries.

Other children at this age who find themselves in similar unthinkable situations may attempt to regain their sense of power by acting out aggressively, becoming very controlling, or behaving confrontationally with peers and/or adults. Whether your child is acting silly or naughty, you can support him with reassurance that such behaviors are normal during scary times. At the same time, it is important to set gentle limits in order to reestablish safety and continuity for your grieving child.

Your Six- to Nine-Year-Old

The world is a pretty scary place, especially when death is added to the mix. If death has touched your child's world at this age, she's probably become very worried. Before, death was merely a concept, and your child may never have considered the notion that it could ever affect her personally, but now that death has become much more real to her, she is very concerned about its implications for her and her family. For instance, if one parent died, then the other parent might also die, and if her friend died then her brother or sister could die, and she could die, too. You can help your child manage these fears by teaching her about the concept of life expectancy.

A little bit of scientific knowledge may calm your child as she learns to face the harsh reality that death eventually touches all of us. You can't make all of her fears go away, but by sharing honest information, your child will begin to process the death more effectively. Tell her that all living things—birds, fish, insects, and people, too—have predictable life spans. Each species has its own unique life expectancy, and people tend to live well into their seventies and often much older. Of course, there are times when people get hurt or become ill. Usually, people's bodies can heal after an injury or illness, and sometimes they take medicine to help their bodies heal. There are even times when a nurse or a doctor is called to help. Sometimes people who are badly hurt or very sick go to a hospital where they are cared for, maybe for a day, sometimes much longer. People who are very sick or badly hurt and are cared for in hospitals usually get better and come back home. There are times, though, when people are so seriously hurt or sick that they die. This is a sad but true fact of life.

As mentioned in Chapter Five, children in this age group will often benefit from knowing that their parents have considered the unlikely possibility that they could die sooner than their normal life expectancy, and have taken appropriate measures to assure that their children will be loved and cared for even if they were to die. If you haven't done so already, prepare a will and make plans for guardianship for your child in the event of your death. Even six- and seven-year-olds who have already experienced a significant loss will typically be grateful to know that you've gone to such lengths to care for them should something happen to you.

Children often figure out more than they are told, so keeping information from them will only increase their fears and their sense of isolation and loneliness. Try using the approach described in Chapter Four: distilling and pacing. Establish a safe environment where you can tell your child the least overwhelming but essential truth. I know that sometimes it may feel as if you're only adding salt to your child's wounds by sharing a difficult truth, but often children already know more than they've been told, and by gently speaking the truth we offer them greater safety and the possibility for having someone to lean on.

I met with Jim, an eight-year-old, who was grieving the death of his cousin while, at the same time, his father was dying in a hospice center. Jen, his mother, started sleeping beside her husband at the hospice, and Jim moved in temporarily with a neighbor. All reports from the neighbor and from Jim's school indicated that he was showing no signs of any serious distress. By the time it became apparent that his father was nearing death, Jim had already stopped asking for visits with him. Jen worried that if she didn't encourage him to visit his father, Jim would regret that he never said good-bye to him. If, on the other hand, he did visit his dad, would seeing him so close to death be too upsetting for him? Given how well her son was dealing with everything, should she avoid telling him that his dad had only a few more days left?

On their way to my office Jen explained to her son that I was someone who helped children and grown-ups who were grieving. Upon entering my office, Jim found art supplies and paper at a

worktable with three chairs. He went right to the art supplies
while Jen and I sat down at the table beside him. After one or two
minutes he snuggled up to his mom and began to whisper something in her ear. She put her arms around him, held him tightly for
a moment, and then said to me, "He wants me to tell him when
his daddy is dying." Jen told him that his father would be dying
very soon, probably in a few days. Later Jen showed Jim a recent
photo of his dad in the hospice, to prepare him for a visit.

As is so often the case, Jen's son knew much more about his father's illness than he was told. He was coping beautifully with the
death of his cousin and with a father who was also dying. Yet
when his mom provided a safe place for him, where he knew they
would both be supported, Jim felt able to ask his mother for more
information about his father's illness and impending death. Once
he was told the truth about his father's condition, Jim chose to visit
his dad at the hospice and say good-bye.

Your Ten- to Twelve-Year-Old

This is an age when children tend to think more and feel less
about death, but they still grieve in their own way. I urge you to
show your child that you respect their process, and to let her know
you'll try to find the answers to any questions about death and
dying she has. Some questions that reflect your child's curiosity
may seem coldhearted. If being asked about the chemicals an em-
balmer uses or how long it takes for dead bodies to decompose are
disturbing inquiries for you, then ask a friend or family member,
or even your funeral director, to speak to your child and provide
these answers. During this developmental stage, you and your child
may be on different bereavement paths, but the more you honor

her questions and concerns, the better she'll be able to manage this difficult time.

Your Teenager

Grieving teens are not always willing or able to communicate with their parents. For instance, some teens may stay out as late as they think they can get away with and once home, avoid eye contact, go straight to their room, slam their door, and turn on the computer. Sandra Fox, a wise teacher of mine, used to suggest that if you face this kind of challenge with your teen, try asking one quick question before the door slams: "Are you talking to anyone?" If the answer is "no," then consider whether your child tends to get through rough times by himself, in which case there may be no cause for alarm. If, however, he is ordinarily a collaborative problem-solver, there may be some cause for concern. In this next anecdote, Phil had stopped hanging out with his friends because he feared that they would misunderstand him.

Six months after his mother died, Phil worried that when he laughed and kidded around with his high school buddies, they would think he had already gotten over his grief and that he was no longer even sad. With adult encouragement, he sat down with his closest friends and explained to them how he'd learned since his mother's death that grief had a way of coming and going, and that he was still grieving a lot even though they might sometimes hang out and have fun.

For many teenagers like Phil, spending time with peers is a high priority, but sometimes they have a difficult time figuring out how to comfortably and safely express their emotions with their friends. Another young man I worked with also faced this particular challenge.

Seventeen-year-old Addison had a passion for street hockey, but after his mother's death, hockey had become risky for him and his buddies because his emotions would get violent and out of control. "Lately," he revealed to me one day, "I have been pounding my friends with my hockey stick! Then I end up apologizing and taking them back to my house, and trying to bandage up their wounds. I end up feeling terrible because I've hurt some guys really badly." With encouragement, he started running track instead of playing hockey, which allowed him to exercise vigorously and even to focus on his anger, while no longer having to worry about taking his anger out on friends. Over time, he found ways of expressing his anger more safely, and could once again enjoy playing hockey.

Since teens often benefit from interacting with their peers, attending a bereavement group is usually the most effective option for them. There are probably a variety of group support options for bereaved teenagers in your community. Contact the nearest hospice or hospital for information. In Part Five I provide guidelines for finding support groups. Bereavement groups held in schools are often the most effective for teenagers because they don't compete with after-school responsibilities and personal interests. Talk to a school social worker or counselor at your teenager's school about this. A mental health counselor or a school-based staff member trained in the area of bereavement should facilitate any group that your child attends.

How to Support Grieving Teens at College

In a conversation I had with David Fajgenbaum, the executive director of the National Students of AMF (Ailing Mothers and Fathers) Support Network, a nonprofit organization dedicated to providing support to grieving college students, it was pointed out that:

- Many college students are struggling to balance their grief with challenging academic expectations.
- Nonbereaved college students are often unwilling or feel incapable of providing support to their grieving friends.
- Since college is supposed to be about "having fun," grieving young people often hesitate to reveal their painful issues.

Fajgenbaum suggested that there are three common concerns among bereaved college students:

1. They feel different from everyone else on campus because they're grieving.
2. They feel helpless. Away from home, possibly for the first time, they are painfully aware that their bereaved family members back home are suffering. If a parent or other significant person is dying back home, they feel powerless to help.
3. They feel guilty. While their siblings and/or surviving parent face all the stress back home, they are removed from everyone and everything, as if nothing were happening. Whether they are partying with their friends, studying for an exam, or writing a thesis, they feel selfish or self-centered.

Here are some concrete measures you can take to help your grieving teen while he is away at college:

- Encourage the student to share his feelings with one or two of his closest friends at school.
- Find out if there are bereavement support services available at the college, and if not, talk to someone at the college counseling center about starting one.
- Suggest that the student go online to the National Students of Ailing Mothers and Fathers Support Network

(http://www.studentsofamf.org) for information about campus support groups for grieving college students.

- Encourage your student to talk with his professors about what's happened. Most professors want to know early on if absences from class are due, for instance, to attendance at a funeral or to traveling back home because of a serious illness in the family. If informed in a timely manner, professors will typically respond appropriately and compassionately.
- If your student is dissatisfied with a professor's response, advise him to talk to the dean of students, who will serve as his advocate.
- If he feels that the institution is still unresponsive, then contact the dean's office yourself. Remember, most professors are put off by direct calls from parents.

Making It Safe to Express Feelings

You can help your child by validating her responses and reassuring her that there are many ways to release her feelings, including playing, singing, and even laughing. Other outlets for your child's emotions can include drawing and painting, organized sports, dancing, playing musical instruments, journaling, and, of course, talking. Tell your child that you understand how valid all of these ways of responding to loss can be.

Like adults, children of all ages need guidelines in order to safely express their grief; otherwise, feelings can become overwhelming. With this in mind, ask your child to agree to these three guidelines:

1. Try hard not to break valuable things while you are venting your emotions.
2. Don't hurt others.
3. Don't hurt yourself.

Sometimes, however, youngsters express their grief in dangerous ways. For instance, when I suggested the above guidelines to Tony, a teenager whose friend was murdered, he replied with defiance.

"That might work for you," he said, "but when I'm really mad, what I like to do is this: First, I make a fist as hard as I can. Then I look for a cinder-block wall or a brick wall and I punch it with all my might. Then I look at my fist—it is aching and bleeding and maybe I broke a bone. I hold up my fist and show it to whoever is around me, and I say, 'See this? This is how I feel!' Now that's com-munication!"

For young people like Tony, big feelings, such as all-consuming rage or deep sadness, often demand demonstrative and dramatic forms of expression, but these young people need to learn to ex-press themselves safely. While Tony's practice of punching the wall and then displaying his bloody fist was certainly a poor choice, he inspired me to introduce to youngsters of all ages what I've come to call "Punch and Show" Bereavement Activities. These activities can empower children to safely express the drama of their pain and suffering.

"Punch and Show" Bereavement Activities for Children and Teens

Before we look at specific activities and games you can teach your child, let's look at some of the reasons for choosing feeling-focused games.

- They help kids practice expressing themselves.
- They don't require that a child have any sophisticated vo-cabulary in order to play.
- They provide a way for young people to contain their big feelings.

- They provide a venue for parents to join their grieving child.
- They provide a platform for young people to safely express and manage feelings that may otherwise overwhelm them.
- They help children and their parents learn to communicate with one another effectively.

With that in mind, consider introducing the following activities to your child.

Beanbag Throw

This game isn't only for the very young and can easily be tweaked for older children and teens. Choose a place where your child can freely and safely throw a beanbag—for instance, at a wall in your home or at a tree outside. Some kids prefer throwing eggs or even rotten tomatoes—outside, of course. Introduce this activity by explaining that sometimes when we grieve, we want to get feelings out by throwing things, and this activity is a good way to vent your feelings safely and appropriately. Encourage your child to make sounds or say words while throwing. If you feel comfortable about it, this is a good time to allow unfiltered expressions of feelings. Your role for this activity is to be a compassionate witness. Even if your child doesn't say anything and simply throws objects silently, your child knows that you are there. All you need to do is offer your praise and be present.

In this next vignette, a bereaved young boy learns about self-expression by throwing beanbags, first in a therapy room and then at home with his mother.

Bobby, a seven-year-old whose father had died, called the beanbags "Rob's mad balls." Each week he raced into my office, went directly to my basket of beanbags, and then vigorously threw them again and again at my office door. Throwing my "mad balls" became his chosen way to communicate angry feelings about his father's death. It felt safe, because I gave him specific guidelines: what he could throw and where he could throw it. One day he invited his mother into a session to show her what he'd been doing. His mother told him how impressed and proud she was that he could express himself so well. During that session, Bobby asked his mother to get him his own set of mad balls to use at home. She agreed and later taped a portion of a wall in their basement for throwing them.

A few weeks later she told me that when she and Bobby returned home with the beanbags, she asked him where he thought they should keep them, and, to her chagrin, he pointed into the living room, at a very fragile, handmade porcelain bowl that was strictly off limits. She took a deep breath and agreed. Then Bobby said, "But Mom, the bowl is so special to you and it could break, so in order to keep it safe, we'll have to keep it out of reach, way up on the highest shelf of the pantry." Mom agreed. She lifted the bowl, Bobby set his mad balls inside, and then he dragged a stepladder over to his mom. Balancing the bowl in her hands, she carefully climbed the ladder, placing it on the top shelf in the pantry. Over the next few weeks, whenever Bobby felt mad at home, he went to his mom and said, "I need my mad balls!" That was their signal to walk together to the pantry. Mom would climb the stepladder and retrieve their now "sacred" bowl. Together they would proceed to the basement, where Mom would ceremoniously set it down on the floor. Bobby would dip his hand into the bowl, pick up his mad balls, and throw them repeatedly at the designated place on the basement wall. Mom would stand by him offering praise and recognition for his ability to express and share his feelings so well. Then they would proceed back to the pantry and return the bowl to its special, safe place.

By choosing to keep his "mad balls" in a porcelain bowl well out of reach, Bobby made sure that his mom would be right there by his side. He seemed to understand that, just like in the therapy room where I was available to be a compassionate witness, he felt best having his mom right there with him at home. Safely throwing objects, whether beanbags, wet sponges, or rotten fruits, can be meaningful for children younger or older than seven-year-old Bobby. Your child, regardless of age, may desire your presence while expressing big feelings. The point is to stay with your child, and, perhaps, to even join in the activity, if that feels right to you.

Scribbling

While scribbling may seem to be a trivial and childish activity, it may actually be a venue for effective emotional expressiveness, especially when a child has had difficulty containing big feelings. Offer your child a large white poster board and challenge her to use crayons to cover all the white space with colors. This is no easy task. The paper itself establishes a boundary for your child and is a metaphor for expressing big emotions without losing control. Some children will boldly take up the challenge; others may want you to join them and help things along. That's what five-year-old Julia asked me to do, so the two of us worked for a long while together, creating our own version of a Jackson Pollock painting.

Julia was the only witness when her beloved neighbor accidentally touched a live wire in front of her home. Following this traumatic death, she underwent a dramatic personality change and became easily provoked. For instance, if a child accidentally brushed up against her in the hall at school, she threw him down and punched him until a teacher pried her off the other child. She frequently shouted profanities at her classroom teacher and was often taken out of school due to severe misbehavior. While Julia and I scribbled together, she talked to me about some of her mad feelings and scared feelings. She scribbled and talked, and the paper itself provided some important, built-in boundaries that made her feelings manageable. Realizing her success, she said to me, "Hey, I can do this when I'm mad!" When she finished scribbling, she leaped up and raced to the waiting room to get her father and brought him into the treatment room. Once they were both inside, she held up her poster board, now richly layered with violently expressive scribbles in a full range of bold colors, and said to her father, "Daddy! This is how I feel!"

Once she felt the success of having completed a feeling-focused activity without getting herself in trouble, Julia's next task was to learn how to express her big feelings appropriately at school, at home, and at other venues. Until now she had only met with failure, but after success with scribbling, she believed it was possible to get her feelings out of her body without getting in trouble.

By the way, some young children scribble so vigorously when engaging in this activity that their crayons break. Comment ahead of time that it's okay if crayons break, just keep on scribbling. Some children have been taught along the way that breaking crayons is a criminal offense, so giving permission to break crayons might avoid unnecessary worry.

Ripping

There is something extraordinarily satisfying about shredding an old phone book with your bare hands. You can feel it in your muscles and see the fruits of your labor in the ink stains that are left on your fingers. Get out an old telephone book and invite your youngster to rip it up. Perhaps you'd like to join him, too.

This activity comes with a warning: This will probably make a mess at home, so carefully choose where your child will perform this activity. When I do this with children in my office, I try to remember to accept that this will temporarily wreak havoc in my space, but that it will be worth the hassle.

Tory was eleven when his father killed himself with a pistol. With a vengeance, Tory danced through my office, ripping, crumbling, and throwing. As I watched him vigorously rip through a thick section of pages, he looked up at me and said, "This is how my heart was ripped open."

After the ripping is over, you may want to suggest that your child pick some of the pieces up off the floor and use them to make a collage to express thoughts or feelings. An art therapist friend suggests that by ripping up colored construction paper along with the phonebook, a child will be able to make a more interesting and expressive collage.

Feelings Vocabulary Games

When I run groups for children ranging in age from six up through teens, I often get out a sheet of newsprint and ask the kids to fill up the entire page with words that convey feelings. Not surprisingly, children often can't get past mad, sad, and happy. Of course, there are lots of other feelings that children struggle with, so I like to help them develop a larger repertoire of feelings words. The following games aid children in finding words to express themselves and, therefore, communicate more effectively.

FEELINGS WALK

Regardless of your child's age, by joining your child in a feelings walk you will help her build a more expressive range of feeling words. In addition, your child will become more attuned to how feelings are communicated nonverbally through body language. Start with a neutral walk. This means that you and your child walk with no particular feeling in mind. Then say, "Freeze!" That means that you both stop in your tracks and wait. Then call out a feeling word that your child already knows and suggest walking with that particular feeling inside you. It doesn't have to show on the outside. Just let it live inside you as you walk together. Then, after a few moments, say, "Freeze!" again. Then shout out a different feeling and walk with that one inside you. To explore more sophisticated feelings, say, for instance, the word *embarrassed*, followed by a brief explanation: "Like when you forgot to bring your homework with you to school." As you play this game, experiment by suggesting that your child can also allow feelings to emerge from the body as he or she walks. For instance, when we're angry, sometimes we stamp our feet as we walk. Or we may walk more slowly when sad. This may lead to a discussion about how we communicate and express feelings through our bodies. Keep going until you or your child want to stop.

With older children and teens, go people watching at a mall or some other location where you can sit down together and quietly observe people walking by you. Quietly discuss how appearances and ways of walking may indicate how people feel inside. Then you might discuss times you might have had or struggled with similar feelings. Also, you may wonder if there were times when others misinterpreted how you were feeling. How did that feel?

GUESS THE FEELING

Decide on a particular feeling you want to explore. Walk into a room and ask your child to guess the feeling inside of you. You might look angry or worried or shy or scared or tired or silly. The point is not for the child to get it right, but to generate more feeling words to add to your list. Often kids want to take turns coming into the room with a different feeling hidden inside of them. This can be a lot of fun!

FEELINGS BEACH BALL

This game is typically appropriate for young children. Write feeling words on strips of paper. Or if your child isn't reading yet, draw feeling faces that express a whole variety of emotions. Tape the strips of paper onto a beach ball. Sit across from your child and roll the ball back and forth. Respond to the word or the feeling face that comes your way either in conversation or by acting out the feeling.

Listening by Drumming

This call-and-response drumming game encourages nonverbal communication. By using drums, tapping on tables, or clapping your hands, send out a rhythm to your youngster and invite him to listen real hard and try to send the same beat back to you. Then he can take a turn, and so on. The beats can be as elaborate as you like. You'll both know that you're really trying to listen to each other.

WHAT TO REMEMBER

In this chapter we examined how children express grief and how you can help your child manage and communicate feelings. As you explore feelings with your child, here are some things to remember:

- Honor your child's way of grieving. Sometimes children feel judged or self-conscious about their grief reactions, so let your child know that you are trying to understand.
- Keep things safe by establishing guidelines for your child's expression of feelings. Remind your child that she can learn to express even her biggest feelings without breaking important things, hurting others, or hurting herself.
- Big feelings may take a lot of energy and physical movement. Children of all ages may respond to throwing and ripping and scribbling, and older children may also find a valuable physical outlet in organized sports.
- Help your child find the most appropriate physical activity to accompany her grief.
- Strive to be empathic and open to your own feelings as you support your child. You don't need to always be the Rock of Gibraltar, and your child can learn much about grief if you are willing to be real with her.

As important as it is to be emotionally honest with your child, be careful not to let your own feelings overwhelm her. Start by listening to your child, and noticing what it is that you are feeling. It may be useful to try imagining a kindly little bird sitting on your shoulder, who keeps a running account of your emotions—now sad, now worried, now irritated—and whispers them in your ear. Since it may be helpful for your child to learn from you that even *your* big feelings are manageable, once you're aware of your emotions, consider sharing them with your child. After you've revealed how you feel, invite your child to share her own emotions. The following strategy can help you learn to attend to your judgmental feelings as you keep on striving to support your child's grieving process.

Maintain Responsible Judgment

As your child grieves, you are likely to become judgmental at times. This would be normal. If you can't stop judging—and let's face it, we're all judgmental from time to time—at least be responsible about it. Take a deep breath and then try to set your judgments aside. Make a conscious decision to curtail all critical comments regarding your child's grief. For instance, don't tell your child to stop feeling so guilty or so angry, or that it is time to stop feeling sad. This won't be easy for you, because you want your child to feel happiness again, and you may believe that it's your job to fix everything for your child. Try to avoid the trap of believing that good parents can fix everything. Your child's grief needs time to heal, and the most effective parents, I believe, give their children the freedom to experience a range of emotions. Tell your child her grief will hurt for a while and that you're going to hang in there no matter what.

Sometimes you need to express your judgments, but never at your child's expense, so find someone—your partner, a trusted friend, or a counselor—you can vent to about your discomfort and your judgments about your child's grief. The next chapter looks more closely at ways of parenting after a death.

∞ 12 ∞

The Parenting Continuum

In Chapter Ten we looked at various styles of grief, such as feeling-focused, action-oriented, getting over it, filling the emptiness, and keeping the connection. There are also various parenting styles that have an influence on families grieving together. Researcher Myra Bluebond-Langner suggests thinking of your own parenting style on a continuum: At one end is a "closed" approach; at the other end is an "open" approach. Open parents are committed to sharing everything with their youngsters because they believe children and teens have the right to any and all information available to adults. Since they can't stop bad things from happening to their children, they can at least try to be open with them, and let them know that they are trusted and will always be given as much control over their own lives as possible. Closed parents, on the other hand, believe, first and foremost, that every young person has the right to be a child. If they can't prevent bad things from happening to their children, then at least they can protect them from having to bear the weight of their difficult circumstances.

Determine Your Parenting Style

Both open and closed parenting approaches are valid and can be equally effective. And like many parents, you would probably place yourself somewhere between the two extremes. To get a clear sense of where you stand on the parenting continuum, ask yourself these questions:

- Do you tend to shelter your child from harsh truths that would affect her life in order to preserve her childhood innocence? If so, you may be closer to a closed parenting style.

- Do you believe that your child has the right to know the truth even if it would cause her to take on responsibilities beyond her years? If so, you are probably closer to an open parenting style.

Once you determine where you would place yourself on the parenting continuum, listen carefully to your child so you can determine if your parenting style is working for your child or if it needs some tweaking either toward more open or more closed. Some indicators from your child would suggest that you shift your position on the continuum in the following ways:

- If your child has been demanding information that you've chosen not to discuss, you might try moving closer to the open style and cautiously providing a bit more information. Remember to pace your conversation with your child. Start by revealing the least overwhelming information as simply and concretely as you can. After allowing her time to digest the information, ask what else she'd like to know. This approach will let her know she's in control, which is important to all children and teens. More information on distilling information and pacing conversations is found in Chapter Four.

- If your child seems to be acting less mature than usual or seems to be uncharacteristically withdrawn or worried, then consider moving more toward the closed style. Start by asking her if you've been telling her a little too much, and if she'd like you to slow down a little. Try letting her choose whether or not to participate in decision making, and ask her how much she'd like to be included. Reassure her that you're willing and able to take care of her and redirect her to more age-appropriate activities so that, hopefully, she'll start to worry less.

Acknowledge Your Own Limitations and Seek Help

During a crisis, we tend to become rigid, and it can be particularly hard to recognize when our children's emotional needs suggest a change in our approach to parenting. However, with patience and some assistance, you can make necessary changes in order to meet your child's needs.

When Geordie was dying from a brain tumor, he boldly challenged his parents' closed parenting style. Eventually they were able to give their son more authority as he died, after one of Geordie's nurses had administered large doses of patience, compassion, and persistence.

Like most parents facing their child's end-stage cancer, eight-year-old Geordie's mother and father struggled to balance desperate hope for a miracle with absolute fear of losing their son. Their approach to parenting involved focusing only on positive thinking, faith, and prayer. Geordie, on the other hand, knew he was dying and wanted to talk about it.

After several weeks in the children's hospital, Geordie grew to understand that his parents couldn't face his persistent questions about death and dying, so he turned to the nurses, and asked them: When will I die? Will it hurt? Is it scary? Will I be alone? They would sit with him and try to reassure him as best they could. However, when his parents overheard one of the nurses talking to their son about dying, they immediately set up strict guidelines for all staff: Always be positive, never talk about death or dying, change the subject if he brings it up.

Geordie would not be stopped. He was an avid reader and had his own Bible with him at the hospital, so he began asking his favorite nurses to read the Bible with him and then discuss particular passages he would choose about death and life after death. When his parents learned what he was up to, his father took an extended leave from work to monitor all staff contact with his son, at which point most of the medical team became frustrated by constraints placed on them. Now Geordie was more and more isolated.

One nurse, however, knew how to address the impasse. Driven by her love for Geordie and concern for his grieving parents, Fran formulated three objectives: Be patient, be persistent, and be compassionate. She patiently listened to their concerns, hopes, and fears. Gradually they got to know and trust her. Eventually they requested that she spend time alone with their son, so she could attend to him in ways they knew they couldn't, even if it meant talking about death with him.

As he lay dying in his hospital room, his mother and father sat by his side, holding a plate of mashed potatoes, Geordie's favorite comfort food. "Eat, Geordie. You need to eat, Geordie. You need to get strong," they told him. Of course, since he was so near death, he could no longer eat anything.

Some staff members were frustrated by his parents' inability to face the reality that their boy was dying, and some nurses believed that the parents were wrong to encourage Geordie to eat. Fran, however, speculated that perhaps Geordie liked having his mom and dad there with him at the end, loving him in their own way and surrounding him with the familiar aromas of his favorite comfort food. After Geordie's death, his parents asked Fran to speak at his funeral and requested that she provide bereavement follow-up support to them.

Looking back, as Geordie pushed for more open communication, his parents became increasingly unyielding in their closed approach to care, which made his last days more challenging for him. Fran's gentle intervention allowed Geordie to have what he probably needed most— consistent, loving, positive parents who were hopeful to the end, and a special nurse who could lovingly listen to him and, against all odds, attend to his emotional and spiritual needs.

Allow Your Child to Establish His or Her Own Terms of Engagement

José's mother had a very open parenting approach as her son was dying. Nevertheless, he struggled to keep his balance and maintain boundaries as he faced death.

I sat in a conference room with José, along with his devoted mother and his favorite nurse, Celine, as José's oncologist explained that all their efforts to fight the leukemia had failed and that José was going to die. The implications of this meeting were profound for all of us.

But as days and weeks went by, he was not particularly changed by the shift to palliative treatment. His conversations with me and with the entire adoring staff were the same. He loved girls and he loved children. He talked about his hopes of meeting a girl and marrying her, and about his plans to someday have a family of his own. José was still very much a "kid." He waited impatiently at every mail call in the pediatric unit for his Make-A-Wish gift to arrive: an all-expenses-paid trip to Disney World for two. José couldn't wait to get on the plane with his mother for that exciting vacation. José also had every intention of moving with his mother to Puerto Rico. Although he was still hospitalized, he reminded his mother not only to pack for their trip to Florida, but also to pack up their apartment and prepare for the big move home to Puerto Rico. José's spirit never waned, as his body became more and more frail. He was too fragile to make the short ambulance ride to his nearby apartment and he would probably die in the pediatric unit in a matter of days.

One day, Celine came to me and said, rather pointedly, "Rob, you're José's grief counselor, is he at least talking about dying with *you?*" The staff looked to me to help José break through the denial and begin to grapple "appropriately" with what was really happening. Everybody, it seemed, was grieving, except José.

I decided to broach the subject directly by saying, "José, we can talk about anything that you want to talk about, but I just want you to know that if you ever want to talk about dying, we can do that, too."

He looked directly at me, and when he spoke, his tone was tough and clear and almost threatening. "Rob," he said, "if you ever bring that up again with me, I'll never talk to you again!"

Message received. I decided to honor José's request, mostly out of respect, but partly, I must admit, because I loved the time we spent together and I didn't want to risk losing any of our precious conversations.

As the days passed, José talked to me, almost exclusively, about his cousins. He was the oldest of several cousins, he explained, and he would miss them when he and his mother moved to Puerto Rico. The move, he explained, would be bittersweet, both a loving reunion and a sad farewell. As he talked of his cousins, I made a list of their names to help me keep track of them all. Then José began to use the list I'd made as he considered which possessions he would leave to each of his cousins before moving. Since he had so many things that he simply couldn't take with him to Puerto Rico, he would have to give something to each of his cousins before leaving. This, then, became the focus of our "grief work" together in the remaining days.

Once, when I arrived in José's room, his face was glowing as he greeted me, waving his airplane tickets. Victory! He was one step closer to his goal. But what José didn't acknowledge was that his body was not cooperating. He could never survive a plane ride.

The last time I saw José, he had been discharged from the hospital. He survived the short ride to his apartment with his mom, and the living room was crowded with moving boxes. His mom had packed for the great move to Puerto Rico, and José was seated in a recliner, emaciated and smiling, holding his tickets to Orlando. They were leaving the next day for Disney World. When they returned, they were moving to Puerto Rico! His emaciated hand swept across the room. "Mom already packed!"

José died that night. Later, his mother told me that his body was shipped to Puerto Rico.

Perhaps there is something to be said for José's denial. Dealing with his death head-on wasn't the way he wanted to experience his last days. He told me that very clearly, once I really listened to him. I knew that he wanted my help organizing his possessions and planning his legacy. That was how I served him in his final days.

Clinging to denial is sometimes the only way we can find to get through unthinkable times. For example, in Shreveport, Louisiana, in the aftermath of Hurricanes Katrina and Rita, I spoke to a chaplain at one of the three main shelters housing twenty thousand evacuees from New Orleans and areas of Mississippi and Alabama. He told me of a man who lost his home and his job, and whose wife and children were still missing. Despite everything, the man seemed to be managing very well, until he lost a small satchel containing a few items he had grabbed from his home before escaping with his life. Empty-handed now, he stood in front of the chaplain shaking uncontrollably, crying like a baby. "With something to hold on to," remarked the chaplain, "he could gracefully endure. But once that satchel was lost, he crumbled." Perhaps the satchel represented hope and the illusion of control in the face of profound powerlessness. A few familiar objects from home may have formed the basis of denial for him.

Like that man in the shelter, Geordie's parents—and perhaps José, too—clung to denial in order to contain the chaos and manage their fears. Unlike Geordie's parents, José's mother and his medical team favored openness and told José that he was dying, but, like the man in the shelter who found dignity by clinging to a satchel, José held on to faith and hope by taking a more measured, metaphorical approach to dying. The closest thing to "death talk" for José was planning a move to Puerto Rico and choosing gifts for his cousins. When I listened to him, our grief work together could begin.

Just like Geordie's and José's parents, you have also had to make many parenting decisions: what to say and what not to say; when to include or exclude your child; whether to empower or protect. You may still find yourself struggling to balance long-standing family traditions with your own and your child's personal needs. Sometimes, in the light of day, you may regret some of the choices you've made. For instance, as you have grappled with your own pain, you may have lacked the energy you wish you had to attend to some of your child's needs. All parents are fallible and sometimes you will need to humbly ask your child for forgiveness. This was the case with Debby and her husband, Joe, who thought they had addressed their five-year-old son's grief after their daughter's sudden death, but thirty years later they discovered they had accidentally let him down.

Debby was distressed by her thirty-five-year-old son's recent revelation that since the age of five, he harbored anger at his parents for barring him from his sister's funeral. Debby tried to explain to her son that his sister was very disfigured in the car accident, and that they thought he'd be traumatized if he saw her in that state. Still, he was exasperated, and asked her, "Why didn't you just keep the casket closed so I could come?"

Debby thought awhile and then replied, "I think it is because we were in crisis. We had to make many unbearable decisions those first few days. Having an open casket is something we just do in our family and it was a tradition we just leaned on without giving it a second thought. But you're right, if we had known better, we would have closed the casket and included you. We are so sorry." All parents are imperfect, and we all sometimes must humbly ask our children for understanding and forgiveness.

WHAT TO REMEMBER

- Learn where you tend to stand on the open-versus-closed parenting continuum. Do you tend to be more unconditionally open so your child will know you trust her to take charge of her own life, or do you tend to put up defenses during tough times to protect your child from truths that could be harmful?

- Watch for clues that might suggest that your child would benefit from your taking a step or two toward a more open or closed position on the parenting continuum.

There are no perfect parents. Now, especially as you grieve with your child, your particular parenting approach, whether open or closed, is probably more rigid than ever. All you can do is be the best parent you can be, mindful that there will be times when the best thing you can do is say you're sorry and ask for forgiveness. That said, if you carefully attend to your interactions with your child, you can strike the right balance on the parenting continuum.

PART FOUR

THE SEARCH FOR MEANING

∾ 13 ∾

Entering the Third Phase
of Your Journey

Up until this phase, your grief has been a process of reacting to loss. During early grief, you and your child were shocked by the terrible news that a loved one had died, and you faced disbelief, anxiety, and numbness. Then, as you encountered the second storm of grief, you and your child learned to manage a broad range of difficult feelings. The pain during the second storm came, in part, as a result of the courage it took to face the depth of your loss. Now, as your journey continues to unfold, you will gradually enter the final phase of grief, a quieter, more reflective path called the search for meaning.

Prepare for a Subtle Shift

If there were a mantra associated with the third phase of grief, it would be: "What is the meaning of my life now that this death has changed me?" Your transition out of the second storm toward a search for meaning will probably be very subtle and involve shifting out of despair and hopelessness into a world of hope and possibilities. Laurie became convinced that her life had become meaningless after her daughter's death, and, therefore, the best course of action would be for her to take her own life. Luckily, she realized that instead of suicide, she could search harder for a reason to go on living.

"The pain after she died was unbearable," she recalled. "I felt isolated and no one understood how overwhelmed I was. I felt helpless and useless and, ultimately, suicidal. I had two other children and, of course, they needed me more than ever, but I couldn't see that at all. So I took a pistol and was about to end my life. Suddenly a fierce voice inside me insisted that there must be a reason to keep living, but that I just hadn't worked hard enough to find out what it was. I was furious because I had made up my mind to end my life and now this voice of hope was throwing a monkey wrench into my plans. I argued with it, but finally it won out.

"I put down the gun and started searching for some new reason to go on living. It wasn't easy. At first I had no idea what to actually do, but in the light of day I realized how I loved working as a nurse. Today I'm employed as a hospice nurse and I continue to love my work. Nursing gives me a reason to live!"

There is a voice within you, too, that is fighting for your life and calling you to discover hope or faith or to seek your higher purpose. For many, like Laurie, who found her meaning and purpose through nursing, this time to reflect will hopefully help you to make changes in your life that will ultimately contribute to your own personal healing.

This is your time to begin reflecting on both what you've lost and what you've gained by the events that have shattered your world. For instance, at this juncture in the journey, you may feel as if one or more significant roles that you've always counted on—brother, sister, son, daughter, partner, beloved friend, or spouse—have disappeared along with the person who died. As a result, you feel stripped of a significant part of yourself, and wonder who you are now.

Consider Who You Are Becoming

As you start to become aware of parts of yourself that seem to have unraveled as a result of the death of your loved one, you may find it helpful to explore more deeply who you are now and how you have changed. In one of my widowers and widows support groups, participants were asked to free associate with pen and paper while pondering the question "Who are you now?" After several minutes to reflect, they shared their thoughts. A widower named Elliott commented that no one in the group had included *husband* or *wife* in their lists. His observation led to a conversation about how empty their lives had become as a result of having lost their cherished designations, husband or wife. One widow revealed that she wanted to put "wife" on her list, but stopped herself because it seemed, somehow, to be wrong to still think of herself in that way. In response to her, several group members reminded her that there were no rules preventing her from putting "wife" on her list, and eventually, with support from the group, she bravely revised her list to include "wife." Interestingly, another member of the group shared how she, on the other hand, felt liberated by choosing not to put "wife" on her list.

Since there are no rules, it may be desirable for you to hold tight to some of your cherished roles, too, but sometimes "holding on" gets complicated. About six months after attending the support group, I heard from Elliott. He had fallen in love again. While his wife was his first love, this new woman made him feel sexier than he'd ever felt before. The problem was that he was feeling guilty, as if he were cheating on his wife and was about to break off the new relationship, but decided to talk to me first. I suggested to Elliott that he talk the problem over, symbolically, with his wife. I pulled up a chair right in the counseling room and suggested that he offer her a seat. He envisioned her in the room, and told her that he'd met someone new and wondered how she felt about it. After a moment's pause, he appeared flushed and his eyes filled up with tears. "I had forgotten until just now," he told me, "that many years ago, before she was even sick, she said that if she were to die first, she hoped I would find someone to love again." Now, with his wife's blessing, Elliott felt free to go forward with his new relationship more easily, without the guilt.

There are lots of ways to communicate symbolically with the dead in addition to the empty chair technique that I used with Elliott. For instance, many people go to the gravesite for a heart-to-heart, or they communicate with their loved one in dreams or in visions. Writing a letter to heal unfinished business can be very valuable, too. A few years after my father died, I completed an exercise in a journaling workshop in which participants were given a sheet of paper with a single vertical line drawn down the center. On the left side, we were invited to write a thought or question to someone absent from our lives. Then, on the right side, we were to write a response, through our own hand. To my surprise, my dad and I had our first of several conversations since his death.

Sometimes, very controlling and dominant partners or parents maintain a strict hold over us, even after they've died. For instance, you may have always wanted to quit your job and go into business for yourself, but your partner insisted that you take a more cautious path, and now, even after her death, you still feel an obligation not to pursue your dream. Or perhaps you always wanted to go back to being an artist, but your father insisted that you take a more traditional route. He still seems to be stopping you, even now. Or it may be something as simple as cutting your hair shorter or growing a beard that seems impossible because of a lingering voice of disapproval. It would seem that you should be freed up now, but you're still feeling held back.

Perhaps a conversation with your controlling partner or parent is in order. Since your relationship may have been unbalanced in the past, think carefully and ahead of time about what you want to say so that you can effectively establish a more egalitarian postdeath relationship. For instance, some questions to consider asking yourself first are:

• What would I like to say to my loved one?
• Are there any specific requests I'd like to make?

A drama therapist once suggested to me that when planning to negotiate with a demanding and powerful partner or parent who has died, picture him "wizened by death." In other words, think of how being dead could be a leveler that has smoothed out some of the rough edges in his personality and, perhaps, even made him kinder and gentler.

Your Deepest Beliefs May Be Challenged

People often say that without faith they could never have weathered the hardships following a death. However, this doesn't mean that you must have religion to grieve well and find peace. For those who don't believe in a God, for instance, leaning on rational beliefs or a faith in the goodness of humanity, or in some existential or moral framework, will often soothe the pain of a loss. Of course, belief in a heavenly reunion or some sort of spiritual embrace often tempers despair, too.

Sometimes death signals a profound spiritual or existential crisis. Your faith can be shattered by death and leave you adrift and unsure of what you believe. You may be left believing that you have lost your God, or that God has betrayed you. If so, you may have entered a struggle to redefine your personal meaning of faith and hope. In the following anecdote, Gloria faced a spiritual crisis that shook her to the core, and it took a spiritually oriented guide to help her begin to reconsider her notion of faith and her relationship to God.

Gloria and her husband, both devout Catholics, had weathered many storms together in their thirty-year marriage, but after her daughter's death, Gloria was suddenly unable to get herself to church. This was very disturbing to her because by entering the church building and participating in the Catholic liturgy with her husband, she felt she was a good wife, a good congregant, and, most important, a woman of faith. Every Sunday after her daughter's death, she walked up to the building arm in arm with her husband, but when they reached the church doors, she became overwhelmed with rage and nausea and had to turn away. She was left believing she'd abandoned her husband, lost the support of her faith community, and failed at her relationship with God. When I met Gloria, her despair was palpable.

"I'm here," she explained, "because I need you to help me get back to church."

Frankly, I doubted whether I would be the right person to assist her in her struggle with Catholicism and faith, and immediately thought of Sister Judy, who epitomized unconditional love and whose sense of humor and compassionate caring were inspirational. I told Gloria that I'd work with her grief, but that I also wanted her to meet with someone in a position of authority within the Catholic Church.

Gloria worked with both of us, alternating from week to week. After her first session with Judy, she looked transformed.

"Everything has changed," she explained. "I told Sister how I felt angry and nauseous at the church doors. When I asked her to help me get back to church, Sister told me that if I never went back into any church ever again, I would still be beloved by God! She said that my rage at God is absolute proof of my faith, and when I turn away I'm not alone. God is there with me. I'm not abandoning my faith, she said. My anger is proof that my faith exists. My job now is to fight with God, and Sister Judy said she'd join me in the fight."

Gloria continued to meet with each of us. Sister Judy, I presume, wrestled with God alongside Gloria, and helped her discover her own spiritual voice. I helped Gloria face her profound pain as a bereaved parent struggling to make sense of a world that had been irrevocably changed.

Once Gloria came to understand that her relationship with God did not require church attendance, her goals in counseling shifted to finding ways to reconnect with her husband and with her faith community without attending church. After several months, Gloria seemed to have made her peace with her God, and became comfortable once again in the church alongside her husband.

God wrestling is a term that captures Sister Judy's work with Gloria. This is sacred work. The best thing I did for Gloria, I suppose, was to help her find the perfect wrestling partner. If you are struggling with your own crisis of faith, if you give yourself permission to rage at God, like Gloria, you will hopefully establish a new, more meaningful notion of spirituality.

WHAT TO DO

Since grief is a lifelong process and the phases of grief are nonlinear, your search for meaning may be difficult to sustain. Reactions to anniversaries such as the date of death and significant holidays will cause you to miss your loved one again and again. Seasons of the year will jar your memory of illness or death. Even celebratory events like birthdays, new births, weddings, and graduations will sometimes take your breath away. A particular time of day may throw you off balance. And new losses and tragedies will occur, causing you to face the challenge of early grief once again. Here are some things you can do to stay on track:

- Set aside five or ten minutes. Sit quietly with a pad of paper and pen and gently ask yourself the question "Who am I now?" Allow yourself to respond honestly in words, phrases, or sentences. Gently repeat the question again and again. Afterward, notice what you've written on your list and what you may have left out. Is there something you'd like to add to your list now? If so, how would that feel? This exercise can also help you identify a valuable internal resource, your own inner observer who can help clarify some of the more subtle dimensions of your loss and some of the inner strengths that you can draw upon as you grieve.
- If you have found that your loved one lingers in ways that are troubling to you, seek healing by having a chat, perhaps even out loud, at the gravesite or at some other special place where you feel his or her presence; asking for a visit in a dream or vision; writing a letter to your loved one to address something unfinished; or having a "conversation" using the split-page technique mentioned above.

• Grief is often a spiritual journey. Have your beliefs been so-lidified or challenged by your loss? If your beliefs are no longer as certain as they once were, and you have been questioning your relationship with God, consider seeking spiritual guidance from a trusted source. I am grateful for spiritual teachers like Sister Judy. However, be wary of others whose rigid interpretations of their particular religion or sect result in punitive and harsh assaults on you as you seek wisdom and peace. Look into your heart and, hopefully, you will find the right spiritual course of action.

∞ 14 ∞

Keeping Your Memories Alive

Once traditional events have ended, you and your child may benefit from informal rituals that will help you continue to keep memories alive. There are various creative commemorations that can help keep lines of communication open and provide a framework for sharing feelings and memories.

Stay Connected with Informal Rituals

In Chapter Six we explored some of the benefits and challenges of traditional death rituals, like wakes, funerals, burials, and memorial services, but there is a whole range of informal ways for you and your child to remember. Here are some ideas for informal commemorations.

PLAN CEMETERY VISITS

Visits to the cemetery with your child can be very meaningful. Talk about your visit ahead of time if you plan on bringing your child with you. Explain why you're going and what will happen

there. If your child is five or younger, remind her that the cemetery has symbolic significance as a "final resting place," but that
being dead is very different from "resting" because being dead
means the body has totally stopped working. Of course, it is important to allow your child, regardless of age, to decide for herself
whether or not she will go.

A bereaved mother named Mandy was convinced that if she
brought Peter, her four-year-old with her to his father's grave, it
would be extraordinarily meaningful for both of them. Mandy's
husband was killed in Iraq by an IED only weeks before he was
scheduled to finish his third tour of duty and return home to
civilian life. It took weeks before his body was finally shipped to
the States and buried near their home. Later, as days and weeks
went by, her husband's grave became her only refuge to unguard-
edly express her deep despair and sorrow. While at the gravesite,
Mandy would sometimes recall how when she was a child grieving her grandmother's death, her grandfather would walk arm in
arm with her to her grandmother's grave and tell loving, unfor-
gettable family stories. Mandy felt inspired by memories of her
grandfather's support, and decided to bring her son, Peter, with
her to his father's grave.

To Mandy's disappointment, Peter agreed to go with her only
once, and then refused to go back without a fight. She tried beg-
ging him and bribing him, but nothing worked, so she started
dragging him into the car as he kicked and screamed. He continued to resist, so she had to pull him out of the car and carry him
against his will to the grave each time they went. Mandy kept
this up for weeks until she realized the problem: Peter had been so
frightened when he saw his mother overwhelmed with grief that
he couldn't tolerate going back there with her. Once she understood this, Mandy stopped taking Peter with her, and eventually,
when he felt ready, Peter went occasionally to the grave with his

grandfather, who displayed less overwhelming expressions of grief.

Mandy knew from her own experience that, under the right circumstances, cemetery visits can be extremely rewarding for children. After her husband's death, however, she came to realize that it was unfair to expose Peter to such an intense level of raw pain and despair. As you consider including your child in cemetery visits, remember that just as children need support at funerals, they need supportive, child-focused adult care at cemetery visits, too.

MAKE A FAMILY MURAL

For families with children eight and older, creating a family mural is an excellent way to explore how your family is changing since your loss. Gather up some crayons and markers and get a large piece of poster board. Then tell your youngster that you'd like to create a picture of your family. John, a father of three boys aged nine, eleven, and twelve, was dying of pancreatic cancer when he and the rest of his family created a family mural.

The boys had been told that their father was dying, but John and his wife, Susan, suspected that it was still all quite unreal to the children, especially since John showed very few outward signs of being ill. The mural project helped them face their painful circumstances with grace and humor.

Clearly they were a family that enjoyed playing together, and as they worked on their mural, the boys started drawing the three of them in a circle, kicking around a soccer ball. Then Susan drew herself alongside the children with a coach's whistle around her neck. Finally, the twelve-year-old wondered aloud where Dad belonged in their picture. After much discussion, they asked John to draw himself jumping on a trampoline, with his arms outstretched, smiling as he waved down to his family. As they worked together on their mural, the boys envisioned themselves engaged in familiar and fun activities even though their world had been dramatically altered; their mother was close by their side in the picture, as their coach available to mentor them during the tough times that lay ahead; and their dad, already on his journey up toward heaven, could still smile down on them and remain connected to his loving family.

Let the mural exercise unfold for you and your child. Be collaborative and have fun. Afterward, talk about what you've created and what you've learned about your family from the exercise.

MAKE A MEMORY QUILT

If you are an able sewer or quilter, you may enjoy designing a memory quilt, perhaps using scraps of material from articles of clothing your loved one used to wear. For a more collaborative, family-focused experience, cut out cotton quilt squares for each member of your family and invite them to create a memory patch for a family quilt. With supervision, younger children can use fabric paints. Older children can be as elaborate as they like. This can be a wonderful way of keeping memories alive.

MAKE A MEMORY SCRAPBOOK

Collect memorabilia such as letters, drawings, photographs, and programs from graduations, plays, or concerts for a scrapbook of family memories. Set aside time to work with your child on this ongoing project.

MAKE A MEMORY JOURNAL

A family memory journal can be as simple as a large loose-leaf book filled with memorable family stories of your loved one. Even your very young child can include drawings and dictate a memory to an older child or adult willing to transcribe it and include it in the journal. You may want to divide the book into sections, and include topics, such as "Funny Memories," "Things She/He Loved to Do with Me," "What I Will Miss the Most," "Things I Never Want to Forget About Him/Her," "Her/His Favorite Foods," and "Her Favorite Sayings or Mottos." You may even include categories such as "Things That Got Me Mad About Her/Him," and sad memories about your loved one, so that you have an honest, well-rounded documentation of your memories. New pages can always be added to this book; if a relative comes to visit who knew your loved one, ask him or her to add memories and stories.

MAKE A MEMORY BOX

Memorial objects don't always fit into a scrapbook or journal. A memory box can hold a lock of hair, a favorite trinket or piece of jewelry, and other three-dimensional objects. You and your child can convert a simple shoe box into a sacred container. Paint the outside of the box, glue on feathers and glitter, or create a meaningful collage. For the interior of the box, line it with velvet or tissue paper to make it special. Take it out when the mood strikes you to start a conversation with your child.

PREPARE A COMMEMORATIVE MEAL

There is nothing like food to bring families together and get them talking. Did your loved one have a favorite meal or some favorite dishes that you recall? If so, a commemorative meal is something you and your child may enjoy planning together.

Before my cousin Anselm died of AIDS, he left specific directions for a special meal to be prepared for his family directly following his memorial service. We stood around a large table weighed down with casseroles, stews, salads, and various desserts. Each item had a card placed in front of it with a story that Anselm had written about a particular memory from his childhood that he associated with the dish. We read and ate and reminisced, and were grateful for the rich sensory experience Anselm gave us.

You can create a meal as elaborate as Anselm's, or simply pass around a bag of popcorn and recall how your loved one could eat one of them in a half hour flat. Either way, food will often elicit memories and bring your family closer together.

SHARE STORIES

Set aside a time for telling family stories, perhaps after a meal, over dessert, or by devoting an evening to storytelling. Seven-year-old Georgia loved to sing and dance. After her father died, she wrote a song in his memory, celebrating the elaborate salads he loved to prepare. She recorded herself singing, choreographed a dance to her song, and performed it for her mother.

After eight-year-old Frankie's father died, he wrote a song called "He's My Dad," which was about his father's many accomplishments and their love for each other. He, too, recorded the song and played it for his mother.

After Georgia's performance, her mother shared some of her own warm memories with her daughter. In contrast, Frankie's mother and father had been divorced, and after his father's death, his mother minimized Frankie's feelings. After listening to Frankie's song, she seemed better able to appreciate the depth of Frankie's grief. Both children found greater intimacy from storytelling. When you are planning to share stories with your child, remember to think outside the box. For instance, if you or your children are dancers, create a dance piece about your memories. If you enjoy singing, write a song that tells your story.

All death rituals are meaningful for both you and your child because they provide opportunities for keeping sacred memories alive. When planning traditional rituals, like wakes, funerals, burials, or memorial services, always insist on them being

family-friendly, and remember to consider a range of informal rituals, too. They will further enrich communication between you
and your child for months and years to come.

In the next chapter, we'll explore times when loved ones seem
to return to us in the form of dreams, visions, or in other unexplainable ways. Some would call these sorts of connections with
the dead spiritual, while others dismiss them as crazy. Known as
after-death visitations, they are not uncommon and can be richly
rewarding, albeit sometimes confusing.

∞ 15 ∞

Unexplainable Visits From
the Dead

A basic concept we associate with being dead is that a person can't come back to life, and in Chapter Five we looked at how to help children grasp the idea that being dead is forever. Still, it is normal and appropriate to want to keep a connection with those who have died. For example, in the last chapter, we examined a whole range of rituals and activities intended to honor and preserve sacred memories. That said, many adults and children report that the dead seem to stay in touch with them, often in the form of waking visions or dreams that are called after-death communications. This chapter explores this concept, and in the Resources you'll find suggested reading on the subject.

When I work with the bereaved, I typically ask whether they've had any sort of visit from the deceased since the death. Once I make it known that I won't judge them for it, I'm frequently told about visions, dreams, and curious visits from animals believed to carry the spirit of a loved one, such as a deer appearing in a backyard, or a butterfly hovering over a garden. Typically, messages from the deceased are loving and hopeful.

After my father's death, I had three experiences where I felt his strong presence. I came away with two lessons from my father's visits. First, I can keep on learning from him even though he is dead. Second, our relationship didn't stop when he died, and it even seems to have improved over time.

My First After-Death Visit with Dad

I was twenty-three when my father died, and completely unprepared to cope. The night after we buried him, I sat alone in my parents' living room, slumped on a couch, deep in reverie. Then, as if in a trance, I stood up and walked over to the bookshelf across the room, and reached for a paperback novel by Herman Hesse called *Knulp*. I had been reading several books by this author, and in an effort to get closer to Dad, I'd loaned him *Knulp* to read. I flipped randomly through the pages until I fixed my gaze on a short passage that read:

I am leaving you now. You must go the rest of the way by yourself.

I closed the book, returned it to the shelf, and went back to the couch. I sat up straight and recited the passage to myself, trance-like, over and over again:

I am leaving you now. You must go the rest of the way by yourself.
I am leaving you now. You must go the rest of the way by yourself.

Gradually I began to understand the literal meaning of the words on the page, which cut me to the quick: I would have to go through the rest of my life without my father. Yet, ironically, it seemed to me as if he were still with me, mentoring me through my grief, and helping me comprehend the immense implications of his death. This paradox, that he was dead but not completely gone from my life, felt comforting to me during early grief.

My Second After-Death Visit with Dad

I have loved music and theater since my childhood, and although my father was supportive of this to a point, he did everything he could to squelch my ambition to make a career as an artist. Finally, eight years after he died, I decided to make the move to New York City to try my hand as a professional actor. I wasn't consciously thinking about my father when I went to bed the night before my big move to New York, but I am certain that he came to me that night when I was awakened out of a deep sleep by his familiar voice shouting out my name. I felt that by calling out to me he'd finally affirmed my dream and blessed my journey.

My Most Recent After-Death Visit with Dad

About fifteen years ago at a family gathering, my brother Cliff walked me to his car, reached into his glove compartment, took out a wrinkled manila envelope, and handed it to me. Inside was a battered black case with Dad's gold watch nestled inside its purple crushed-velvet interior. I was flooded with memories.

My father had always been a very capable and responsible man. He had courage, confidence, smarts, and creativity. For Dad, being on time represented being on task, available, and reliable, and staying on top of important and pressing matters. So of course when I reached adolescence, he always wanted me to wear a watch. For me, back then, watches represented the rigid, uptight world of adulthood, so I stubbornly refused to wear one, and it was long after Dad's death that I made my uneasy peace with time and came to rely on a wristwatch to help organize my adult life.

As I held Dad's gold watch in my hand it felt as if I had come full circle. I reverently took off my cheap Timex and slipped on Dad's gold beauty. I loved how it gently gripped my wrist. It was solid and reliable—like Dad.

I put on the watch each morning. It became my new spiritual practice. Unfortunately, though, it kept lousy time. I'd had unreliably slow watches before, but Dad's ran very fast. Within a single hour, it raced ahead—first one, then two, and sometimes three hours ahead of itself. On some days I could actually see the hour hand moving on the watch face. Somehow, I believed that it just needed some time to get back on track and I resisted taking it in for repair for a long time. Instead, I compensated for my slight handicap by continually asking my clients and colleagues for the correct time.

Eventually, after searching for a shop that was both reliable and trustworthy, I chose the oldest jewelry establishment in the city to repair the watch. The jeweler, an elderly man with thick glasses, stood behind a cold marble counter as I took off Dad's watch. He reached out and in one swift motion took it, dropped it in a small white envelope, and handed me a pink slip of paper. I felt naked without it.

A week later, I returned to the store and passed the slip to the watchmaker. He hummed softly to himself, rummaged through a very stuffed drawer, and finally held up the watch. "Oh yes . . ." Then he fell silent a moment, cleared his throat, and muttered, "I'm sorry, but this watch can't be fixed."

"What do you mean?"

"A beautiful old watch. Old . . . I'm afraid that if I opened it up to examine the insides, it would more than likely fall apart, right in my hands. It would self-destruct, so to speak . . . it is simply too risky to proceed."

"But this was my father's watch! You have to fix it!"

"Well," he advised, handing it back to me, "start thinking of it, instead, as if it were a piece of jewelry and not a timepiece. Get yourself a more reliable watch to keep time, but wear this one on special occasions, as a memento or keepsake."

I was defiant! "No. I'm going to wear this watch, and it will work!"

Feeling slightly foolish, I stormed out of the store, stood on the sidewalk, and slipped the watch onto my wrist. The oddest thing was that it immediately started telling the correct time, as if Dad were smiling down at me and zapping his watch back into shape. But several months later, after keeping perfect time, it must have grown tired, because it stopped working for good. When I noticed that it had died, I put it away in my dresser drawer, where it remains to this day.

I'll never forget how good it felt finding Dad's watch after so many years and how much I loved wearing it, whether it worked or not. Maybe at the very moment that I declared my blind faith in the old watch, Dad and I had finally finished our battle over time versus spontaneity. I've had several watches over the years, yet I still take out Dad's watch now and then. When I hold it in my hand, it still feels good.

If you have encounters with your loved one, as I have had, they may offer you opportunities to better understand and appreciate your relationship with the deceased. In my own case, every time my father seemed to visit me, I learned something valuable. The first time, I felt he was mentoring me through the shock of early grief, helping me understand the finality of his death and also the possibility of continuing our relationship. In the second

visit, I felt that Dad was letting me know that he had stopped interfering with my true purpose in life. Finally, in his last visit, it
felt as if he were playfully helping me trust that as I matured
through adulthood, I would never forget him.

Two Common Responses to After-Death Visits

From my own conversations with bereaved children and adults,
I've found that grievers tend to react to these sorts of unexplainable connections in one of two ways: Either they find them
helpful on their grief journeys, or they find them confusing and
upsetting. Let's examine these two responses:

- Typically, visits with the dead feel positive and affirming,
  and contribute toward healing unfinished business. For instance, loved ones who return after a painful death sometimes
  reappear whole, healthy, and free of pain, and advise the
  grievers to stop worrying about them. Encounters like these
  typically feel special, spiritual, reassuring, and comforting. If
  you've had this experience, consider sharing your story with a
  relative or friend whom you can trust to be respectful and affirming.
- You may have a visit that is disappointing, confusing, or even
  uncomfortable. Perhaps you're waiting impatiently for a reassuring sign or message from the dead that has not yet come,
  or a friend or relative has had a dream or communication
  but you haven't, and you feel rejected. Or maybe a visit left
  you feeling uncomfortable and confused because it was something you neither expected nor desired. If you've had this
  sort of uncomfortable experience, try telling your story to
  someone who is nonjudgmental and respectful. I'm often
  told that when people are paid attention to, they're relieved

of some of the loneliness. Hopefully, in time, you will discover meaning and value from your experience.

Whether you believe death to be final or not, you or your child may experience a connection with the dead. Be open to each other, and if it feels right, tell your child the story of a visit you've had. Then listen to what your child has to say. Wonder together about the meanings you both can derive from your experiences, and remember to normalize this phenomenon with your child.

A Writing Prompt

Write a letter to the one who has died expressing your appreciation for staying in touch, or ask for a helpful message or visit.

∞ 16 ∞

"Finding Peace" for You and Your Child

Learning to move forward after loss is more about finding peace than about establishing closure. Perhaps, as you read this chapter, the crisis in your life seems to have subsided a bit and you've already begun to find your stride again, or maybe you're still right in the thick of disruptive and painful feelings, so the notion of healing or moving on seems very far off to you. Either way, how you move on will reflect how you've been living out your grief, and although grieving may end someday, healing will surely take a lifetime.

Why Making Peace with Loss Is Complicated

The grief journey takes many twists and turns, even in its final phase. One reason for this is that each single loss may have many far-reaching implications. For instance, if an elderly parent or partner dies from a chronic illness, the death may trigger feelings of emptiness and role confusion for the bereaved person left behind; or if a spouse or parent who was abusive dies, the death may trigger grief over the loss of a relationship that was never achieved. Grief from these second-tier losses can be as great or greater than the death itself.

Remember, also, that grief is not limited to death loss. Other, more subtle losses take us by surprise and add to the challenge of moving on. For instance, as you're celebrating your wedding, you may grieve for your loss of independence. As you take pride in a job promotion, you may realize how much you'll miss your office mates. At your child's graduation from college, you may feel nostalgia for the baby you once held in your arms. These smaller pangs of sadness or regret sometimes remind us of our grief for our greater losses, too.

Even more troubling kinds of grieving occur when the world seems shattered by unexpected nondeath events. For instance, you may grieve when a significant relationship comes to an end, if you lose your job, if your child is born with a serious birth defect, if you are displaced from your home after a disaster, or if you are diagnosed with a chronic health condition. Be careful not to give these nondeath losses short shrift, for they deserve your attention, too.

There are also anniversary reactions to be reckoned with. These may be memories associated with birthdays, the date of a death, significant holidays, a particular season of the year, or even a particular hour in the day. Often it is helpful to anticipate specific times or dates, and decide ahead of time how you're going to mark those occasions. Some families bake a cake on the birthday of a loved one and reminisce around the table. Others purchase a gift they would have given to the person who died but present it, instead, to a charity. Some families create new traditions for holidays that were closely associated with their loved one. For instance, on Thanksgiving they choose to help at a food pantry instead of sitting down at a traditional meal, or on Christmas they decide to travel to a warmer climate to avoid memories associated with a white Christmas. Some families choose to hang a Christmas stocking for a beloved family member who has died, and invite friends and members of the family to write memories on a piece of paper to put into the stocking instead of the usual stocking stuffers. Then, on Christmas day, they read the collected memories. Sometimes, despite all your efforts, an anniversary reaction takes you by surprise, but usually you'll be able to plan ahead and reduce some of the shock associated with triggering times.

In addition to the second-tier losses, nondeath losses, and anniversary reactions that reactivate grief, you will also, invariably, be challenged when new deaths throw you back to early grief and the second storm. For all these reasons, making peace with your loss is going to be complicated.

What Makes the Healing Process Particularly Hard for Children

Throughout this book, you've learned how to assist your child through the grieving process. Now it is time to help her learn about finding peace. First, let's review some of the unique features of childhood and adolescent grief:

- Many children weave in and out of their pain more rapidly than adults, whose feelings often linger much longer.
- Children often look as if they aren't grieving because they're playing or laughing with their friends.
- Children have developmental limitations that will delay their ability to fully understand what loss means.

- Children often don't have the words to describe their feelings of grief.

As your child grows and advances through the developmental stages described in Chapter Five, she will reexperience loss again and again, but from a more and more mature perspective. For instance, as your child feels the absence over time of the person who died, she'll gradually know that being dead is very different from simply leaving for a while and coming back later. Her deeper understanding of what death means will renew her pain associated with the loss. In addition, as she begins to grasp the idea that everybody will someday die, her grief will mature and be reintroduced. And as she becomes less reliant on magical thinking, she'll begin to face more of the risks and fears associated with death. Some would say that grief extends longer for young people, because their appreciation for what has happened takes more time to develop. Due to all these factors, it is easy to see why finding peace will be different for your child, and perhaps even more challenging than for you.

How You Can Help Your Child Find Peace

All along we've looked at the importance of being available to your children as a mentor through challenging times after death. Now that she is learning to come to terms with her loss, your child needs you again. There are specific ways that you can help.

BE AN ADVOCATE FOR YOUR CHILD

Now that you have a better understanding of grief, your child needs you to spread the word to others in her life. Talk to her classroom teachers, Sunday school instructor, team coach, minister, and any other significant adults about what you're learning about childhood grief. For instance, explain that it is normal for children to grieve differently from adults, and that even if your child appears not to be grieving, she still is. Tell them that for years after a loss, your child is likely to still have new pangs of grief as she grows up and understands more of what she's lost. Explain that there will be triggering times in your child's life that could easily be missed unless adults are vigilant. Tell them to be patient and compassionate at school, and explain that your child's academic success may suffer for a while as she adjusts and readjusts to her loss. As your child advances through school, remember to inform new school personnel about your child's loss history, because even though time will pass, childhood grief typically lingers.

MAKE A CIRCLE OF GRIEF

Like adults, children also face emotional triggers that can be confusing and overwhelming to them. By letting your child know about triggers and helping him anticipate the surges of grief that come with them, your child will better understand that discovering peace doesn't mean having to finish up his grief. The Circle of Grief will help you explain triggers to your child and teach him to manage them effectively. To make a Circle of Grief with your child, draw a large circle on a piece of paper, then draw two lines to divide the circle into four equal quadrants, each of which will represent a season of the year. With your child's help, try remembering all of the significant times in your lives—birthdays, holidays, anniversaries, dates of deaths—and mark each special time within the appropriate quadrant of your circle.

If you notice that your child has begun to regress, is more irritable than usual, or has been falling behind in school, search the circle for a clue to the problem by checking the quadrant that represents the current season of the year and look for any significant events there. If you find something, it may be the trigger that has been causing your child's distress. Once you and your child begin identifying triggers this way, emotions will become more understandable and predictable. For instance, if you come to understand that tempers flare at home when you're approaching your wife's birthday, you can remember to talk it over ahead of time and to practice patience and understanding with each other.

SHARE "TEACHING STORIES" WITH YOUR CHILD

We are all—adults and children—drawn to stories about real people who've faced great challenges in their lives. For this reason, I've shared many stories throughout this book intended to teach and inspire. Here's how I used to share one of my own personal stories about going through grief with my daughter when she was a small child:

> Eleven years after my dad died, I remember holding you when you were just born. As I looked into your beautiful brown eyes for the first time, I felt ecstatic. I was still elated when, later that same day, I left you and Mommy at the hospital to pick up some supplies from home. I felt as if I were floating through the city on pure joy as I rode in the taxi to our apartment building. Then I took the elevator up to the twenty-first floor, fumbled with the keys, and finally entered our apartment. When the door shut behind me, and I was finally alone in the silent entryway, I fell to the floor and began to weep for my father, who, I suddenly realized, would never know the sweetness of his first grandchild; for you, who would never feel your grandfather's rough beard and kind kisses; and for myself, who would somehow have to figure out on my own how to be a daddy.

While my story is sad, it tells of a never-ending love between children and their parents, and demonstrated to my daughter how major life events, like births, can sometimes be bittersweet. Our teaching stories grow out of our life lessons, and you, too, have valuable stories waiting to be told to your child. To find them, set aside a solitary evening, sit quietly with a pad of paper and pen, and try responding to these sentence starters:

- I was deeply challenged when . . .
- I remember being terribly disappointed after . . .
- I learned how it felt to be absolutely vulnerable when . . .
- My crisis of faith came when . . .
- It was clear what I had to do after . . .

Hopefully, these writing prompts will encourage you to reflect on some of the lessons you've learned throughout your life. Once you've finished responding to them, gently ask yourself the following questions:

- What was the hardest lesson I've ever had to face?
- Did someone help me? Or was I on my own?
- What surprises me again and again?
- What do I keep forgetting but need to remember?
- What have I learned from my past mistakes?
- Over the years, who have been my greatest teachers?
- What keeps me going despite everything else?
- What do I want my child to know that has helped me the most?

Now that you've taken time to consider some of your greatest challenges and most important life lessons, look for stories from your life that you'd like to share with your child. There may be one or many stories that stand out for you. Storytelling can be totally spontaneous or it can become a family-time ritual. Remember that like any good story, finding just the right time to share it often increases its effectiveness. Some will mean more to your child when she's young; others will be best saved until she's older, when she's more ready to hear what you have to say. You'll probably share some stories with your child only once, but others are likely to become favorites that you'll repeat again and again.

Finding Peace Is Not About Forgetting

Make it a point to talk about those who have died. Say aloud the name of the person who has died. Incorporate memories into the fabric of your lives. And tell your child that it is okay to be happy again and to look forward to life, even without her loved one.

PART FIVE

SEEKING
PROFESSIONAL HELP

∾ 17 ∾

Getting the Help You and
Your Child Deserve

Even though grief is a normal and predictable reaction to loss, there are times on the journey when you would benefit from professional therapeutic support. For instance, if grief seems unending and disabling for you and/or your child, grief counseling can help you learn to live fully and grieve more effectively.

What Is a Grief Counselor?

There is no licensing requirement for being a grief counselor, so anyone can call him- or herself one. However, when choosing a grief counselor, you can narrow the process by selecting from a range of licensed mental health professionals who offer grief counseling. These may include licensed professional counselors, social workers, psychologists, and marriage and family therapists. Or there are also clergy and pastoral care professionals who specialize in grief counseling. However, don't assume that every licensed mental health professional or clergyperson has expertise in grief counseling. In fact, many masters and doctoral programs in psychology and many seminaries have little or no course work in grief counseling.

In the last few years, more and more helping professionals have become certified as grief counselors through the Association for Death Education and Counseling (ADEC), an international organization devoted to enhancing the study of death, dying, and bereavement. ADEC offers two certifications, the CT, which stands for certified thanatologist, and the FT, for fellow in thanatology, which indicates a greater degree of experience and expertise in the field. Both the CT and FT mean that the person has undergone specialized education in thanatology, the study of death, dying, and bereavement. Therefore, the CT or FT, in conjunction with a license indicating counseling expertise, offers some assurance that a prospective counselor has training and expertise in the field of grief.

Since choosing the right helping professional for you and your child can be confusing, here are some questions to ask a prospective grief counselor to help you in making your choice:

- Are you licensed to provide counseling?
- What kind of experience do you have providing grief counseling?
- Are you comfortable working with people facing illness, death, and grief?
- Are you a certified thanatolgist or fellow in thanatology?
- Do you have expertise in providing grief counseling to both children and adults?
- Do you work from any particular religious or spiritual orientation?

Find a Grief Counselor Near You

There are various ways to find a grief counselor near where you live. If you prefer a personal referral, start by asking a friend, a clergyperson, or your family doctor to recommend someone. Since hospices typically have referral lists of grief counselors in private practice, you could also contact a hospice near your home and request a referral.

When to Seek Professional Support for Yourself

There are two reasons to consider seeking professional bereavement support. First, the circumstances of your loss are so extraordinary that professional assistance is advisable; and second, the degree of pain you are experiencing is so intense and prolonged that you're no longer able to function effectively. Let's examine each of these situations.

EXTRAORDINARY CIRCUMSTANCES

Your decision whether or not to seek assistance from a grief counselor or other helping professional is a very personal one, and you don't need to fit into any of the following categories to warrant your seeking professional support. However, since the circumstances tend to be especially difficult for many grievers, you can use the list that follows to help you decide whether or not to seek professional help.

Death of a child: The death of a child is a parent's worst fear. This is a life-changing loss that typically remains all-consuming for a very long period of time. It often sets into motion a range of challenges including immobilizing grief and heightened marital stress. Siblings of the deceased child require attention and loving support, but they often feel abandoned by their parents. For all these reasons, when a child dies, grief counseling can be invaluable. In the next chapter we'll look at various support groups, including Compassionate Friends, a self-help organization for bereaved families after a child dies.

Multiple deaths: When many people die, for instance from an epidemic or due to an accident, it may seem as if the dead are competing for your attention, and your grief may grind to a halt. Grief counseling can help you manage this great challenge and help you decide how best to begin your journey.

A sudden death: When you've had no time to prepare and no opportunity to say good-bye, grief can be particularly disruptive and shocking. A grief counselor can help you manage the chaos and start to deal with unfinished business.

Violent death: Grief following a traumatic or violent death such as suicide or homicide often gets complicated. Your reactions may seem confusing and illogical. Your ability to hold on to memories may seem compromised. Perhaps you are unable to enjoy reminiscing about the person who died, or you can't stop thinking about the death.

While eventually you will become able to access pleasurable memories about the person who died, right now you may be consumed by any of three clusters of symptoms that are often experienced after a violent death: reexperiencing, avoidance, and hyperarousal.

- Reexperiencing is a form of reliving the trauma. You may have all sorts of sensory intrusions—sights, smells, or sounds, flashbacks, intense emotions, and nightmares—that demand all of your attention and frighten you. You may be fixated on images and memories associated with the actual death, and you may blame yourself or others for what has happened.

- Avoidance involves staying away from certain people, places, and things that you associate with the death in order to keep from having flashbacks. As a result, you may find that you're blocking out all memories of your loved one, even the positive ones.
- In a state of hyperarousal, you are unusually jumpy. You can't seem to settle down, and you feel generally unsafe most of the time.

As troubling as these symptoms of traumatic grief are, they are quite normal given the circumstances, and you can eventually begin to feel less entrapped by the trauma. Seek out a helping professional who has expertise in both trauma treatment and bereavement.

WHEN YOUR REACTIONS ARE EXTREME

Another way of determining whether or not to seek professional help is by considering how you've been handling your various grief reactions. Throughout this book I've emphasized how normal grief can be excruciatingly difficult. There are, however, times when grief is so overwhelming and prolonged that it becomes especially problematic. With this in mind, if any of the following reactions persist beyond six months and *they seem to be interfering with your ability to function in the world*, it may be time to talk to a grief counselor:

- You can't stop yourself from thinking about the deceased, and these thoughts are interfering with your ability to relate to others and/or function at work.
- Your yearning or searching for the person who has died is compromising other relationships and/or interfering with your job.

- Your loneliness has become impossible for you to tolerate.
- Your life feels entirely empty and meaningless, making it impossible for you to look forward to anything.
- You feel numb or detached from the rest of the world and can't relate to others around you.
- Well beyond early grief, you continue to disbelieve that the death has happened.
- Your anger, irritability, and/or bitterness are compromising your relationships at home and your ability to function at work.

Always seek professional support if:
- You have persistent thoughts of hurting yourself or others.
- You are abusing alcohol or other substances.

We've just looked at two ways to determine when to reach out for professional assistance for yourself, but children sometimes have special needs as they cope with loss, too. Now let's look at how to tell if your child needs professional help.

When to Seek Counseling for Your Child

For a variety of reasons, grieving children sometimes have special needs and would benefit from professional help to supplement the loving care their families provide for them. In the next anecdote, a concerned parent raised this very issue at a community meeting at her daughter's elementary school, following the death of the school principal.

A team of staff members assured parents at the meeting that the crisis had been handled well and all students were now safe and felt protected. But a mother of a student stood up and said, "I am grateful that you responded so well to this incident, but now that the dust is settling, how do you know which children will need additional help managing their grief?" Her question was timely and it prompted the school to explore three areas of concern: How are the students expressing their grief? Do any children have special circumstances that are complicating their grief? Were any students exposed to the actual death? These same three areas of concern will help you determine whether or not your child may have special bereavement needs.

Explore How Your Child Expresses Her Grief

It is normal and desirable for your child to learn how to manage and express a broad range of grief reactions, such as sadness, guilt, anger, apathy, and anxiety. Sometimes, though, children have difficulty managing their feelings. Since you know your child better than anyone else, your own impressions and observations of how she is grieving are very important. Take time to closely observe your child's grief reactions. If at any time you suspect that her grief seems particularly intense, prolonged, or unusual, consult a grief counselor. For instance, you may notice that your child seems unusually submissive or appears to be in shock, or has turned inward and seems numb or immobilized. Perhaps, on the other hand, she seems unusually aggressive and out of control. These reactions could suggest that your child would benefit from grief counseling.

In general, if you're not sure about what you see, trust your gut and talk to a professional about your concerns. There are certain red-flag reactions, though, that call for an immediate referral to a helping professional:

- If you have any concerns about suicide risk.
- If you see evidence of any self-harm occurring, such as cutting parts of the body.
- If your child is behaving violently toward others.
- If you suspect that your child may have an emerging eating disorder or a recurrence of an eating disorder.
- If you suspect any substance abuse, including alcohol use.

Don't hesitate to seek professional advice if you have any of these concerns.

Consider Other Life Circumstances Affecting Your Child's Grief

Nobody experiences loss in a vacuum. Your child is grieving within a larger context that may be particularly challenging and require additional support from a professional. Talk to your child about her concerns and consider seeking additional help. The following questions can help you identify some possibly complicating situations:

- Have there been any significant past losses or traumas in your child's life prior to this current event? If so, grief from past losses or traumas, even from many years back, may resurface now and overwhelm your child. Talk to your child about it and consider getting additional help.
- Does anyone close to your child have a serious illness? If so, a new death in her life may cause her to become anxious. She may benefit from counseling support.
- Does your child have a loved one in harm's way, for instance, in the armed services? If so, this could easily heighten your child's anxiety and compound her grief.

- Is your child developmentally disabled? If so, she may not be getting all the help she needs to understand the meaning of death. Consider a professional consultation.
- Does your child have a serious physical illness of her own? If so, your child's own end-of-life concerns can complicate her grief reaction. You may want some assistance talking to your child about this.
- Is your child already in counseling for another emotional or psychiatric problem? If so, talk to your child's counselor about how her particular psychological issues might be challenging her grief. Ask how this is being addressed in her therapy and how you can help.

Determine the Degree of Exposure to Death

Direct exposure to a death can cause a traumatic grief reaction. The symptoms of traumatic grief discussed earlier apply to children, too, but children typically express themselves differently from adults and therefore present unique challenges. In this next example, eight-year-old Jonah was waiting for the school bus early one morning when it suddenly skidded on some black ice and flipped over right in front of him.

Several children were thrown onto the street, and later Jonah learned that one child died. Jonah's whole body froze up as he watched the events unfold. The police arrived, followed by the emergency medical team and several ambulances, but no one noticed Jonah. After they had all left the scene, Jonah felt as if he couldn't move. It took several attempts, but eventually he could raise his arms, lift his legs, and somehow get himself to school.

Jonah would have benefited from trauma therapy to supplement the bereavement support made available to the students at his school, but unfortunately, it took him several years before he could tell anyone that he'd even been at the scene. In the meantime, he faced the three symptom clusters of reexperiencing, avoidance, and hyperarousal. Without appropriate help, Jonah suffered needlessly.

If you suspect that your child was directly exposed to a death, have him evaluated by a grief counselor who specializes in childhood traumatic grief, even if your child seems to be doing fine. Sometimes when children are indirectly exposed to a death, they have trouble coping, too. For instance, in addition to Jonah, who had difficulties due to direct exposure, another child, who was home sick on the day of the accident and was spared direct exposure, was also traumatized because of his strong affinity with friends on the bus. Since it is hard to predict how children will react to various degrees of exposure to a death, here are some symptoms that can help you identify possible childhood trauma reactions:

- Regression (in young children this may include bedwetting, fear of sleeping alone, and increased separation anxiety; older children may become clingier and act less mature).
- Talking obsessively about the incident.
- Difficulty focusing on academics.
- Fear of the incident reoccurring, despite reassurances to the contrary.
- Anger that seems to spill out inappropriately.
- Self-destructive behaviors, like cutting parts of the body or abusing substances.
- Persistent self-blame.

Regardless of how your child responds to loss, if you know that she witnessed the death, don't wait for symptoms before you consult with a child bereavement specialist. In the meantime, here are some concrete things you can do for your child:

FOR YOUR PRESCHOOLER OR KINDERGARTNER
- Maintain routines like bedtime, mealtimes, story time, etc.
- Offer plenty of reassurance and safety.
- Encourage verbal and nonverbal expression.
- Provide plenty of opportunities for fine and gross motor activity and age-appropriate play, and a full range of opportunities for creative expression.
- Enrich your child's "feelings vocabulary."
- Offer clear, concrete, and simple answers to all of your child's questions.

FOR YOUR ELEMENTARY SCHOOL CHILD
- Follow suggestions for preschoolers and kindergartners.
- If trauma reactions interfere with academic performance, encourage school personnel to reduce academic requirements for a while.
- Look for opportunities for your child to help other children in need.

FOR MIDDLE SCHOOL AND HIGH SCHOOL YOUNGSTERS
- Follow suggestions for elementary school children.
- If appropriate, provide opportunities for your child to participate in community recovery efforts.

Since children often have difficulty responding to traumatic situations, caring adults can play a very important role in children's lives as they recover from traumatic grief. I had a very moving experience counseling a group of twenty youngsters ranging in age from two to seventeen, many of whom witnessed their uncle kill himself with a gun during a family party—after he had left his own apartment, where he'd murdered his wife in front of his two daughters. One week after the murder/suicide, I was summoned to the children's grandmother's parlor, where they were crowded together sharing in their grief. The boys and girls were back at the scene of the suicide, waiting for my guidance.

As I entered the parlor, I noticed that some children appeared to be very numb, as if they were in a trance. They sat on the floor or paced very slowly, detached and isolated from others in the room. Some children ran about with tremendous energy. Some looked frightened and others agitated. There were children crying inwardly and others crying out loud. One little girl stood in a corner of the room, and with her index finger up to her forehead, simulated pulling the trigger of a gun over and over again. She kept shooting herself, falling down, and standing up again. Another child wept loudly with absolute abandon, crying desperately for her mother, while an older child cradled the girl in her lap. These were the two girls who had witnessed their father kill their mother only hours before he killed himself.

Their grandmother and I stood watching the children at the doorway to the parlor. She seemed to be waiting, perhaps for them to notice us and quiet down. After a few moments, they became very still, all eyes now on their grandmother and the grief counselor.

"This is Mr. Rob," she told them, "and he's here to speak with you."

She turned and left the room, closing the pocket doors behind her.

The children quietly looked at me. I took a deep breath, looked around the room, and spotted a stuffed armchair. I crossed over to it and turned to face the children again.

"Would you like to hear a story?" I asked.

All heads nodded affirmatively.

"Okay. I'll put these art supplies in the center of the room. You can share them. Here is some paper. You may write or draw while I read aloud to you."

They took directions beautifully, yet I had serious doubts about the book I had with me. *Tell Me, Papa,* by Joy and Marv Johnson, is an excellent children's book about death and funerals, but I had expected to be meeting only the two girls whose mother was murdered, and not twenty children from two to seventeen. Since I didn't know what else to do, I sat down and started to read aloud. The book captured everyone's attention. They all leaned in close and busily wrote or drew as I read. When I had finished, a hush had fallen over the room. Quietly, they sat and waited.

Then, out of the silence, one of the older boys spoke up.

"Read it again, please."

I wasn't at all certain about the wisdom of reading it twice, but the consensus in the room was that I should. So, somewhat reluctantly, I read again. First, I gave out more paper and suggested again that they write or draw as I read to them. The kids formed a tightly knit circle on the floor. The littlest children curled up alongside their older cousins or siblings. One young child crawled into my lap. Despite my earlier reservations, the second reading went very well.

Once finished, they all stood up and formed a circle around me. They took turns sharing their drawings, letters, and stories. The younger ones had drawn flower gardens and rainbows. The older ones wrote stories about memories of their mother or aunt. Then, one by one, they handed me their creations. There was a respectful hush in the room as one of the children spoke up.

"You'll be there tomorrow, right?"

"Yes," I replied. "I will see all of you at the funeral tomorrow."

The next day I was running late. I raced through the church parking lot and could hear the organ playing. Damn! The service had already started!

I opened the great, creaky front door of the church and stepped inside. The large lobby was empty except for a teenager

I'd met the day before, standing at the doorway to the chapel. He looked my way and we waved. I walked up to him, and we nodded to one another. Then he turned, looked inside the chapel, and started making a funny little hand signal. When I looked where he was signaling, several of the children from the day before were craning their necks, looking for that signal that told them I had kept my promise and gotten there. Apparently, that teenager by the door had been chosen to wait outside the chapel to signal my arrival.

There are several lessons to be drawn from this story that will, hopefully, help you feel better prepared if you have a child who was exposed to a traumatic death.

Provide concrete information: Even if the trauma seems to be more pressing than the death itself, children need practical information. Bringing *Tell Me, Papa* helped me provide details about the meaning of death and about the funeral. If they had needed to be told about the murder and suicide, I would have used the distilling and pacing strategies described in Part Two of this book.

Provide a creative outlet: Coloring, sketching, or writing can be helpful for children of all ages as they process difficult information. Avoid telling your child what to write or draw. Instead, give her lots of options. That way she'll know that you trust her to make good choices.

Be flexible: When the children asked me to read the story again, I did, despite my reservations, and it paid off. The more you trust your child, the more he'll trust you. As important as it is to have a plan, be ready for the unexpected and try to listen to what your child needs.

Create a calm atmosphere: The children seemed to settle down quickly when I read to them. If your child loves to be read to, a story time may provide just the right atmosphere for addressing the difficult subject matter at hand.

Keep your word: Even though I arrived late for the funeral, it was essential that I showed up. Don't make promises to your child that you can't keep.

WHAT TO REMEMBER

Remember to listen closely to your child. He may become your teacher as you begin to find peace together. Reassure your child that you will do all you can to take care of him and that you'll be there for the long haul.

Provide appropriate limits for your child, but also be sure to give honest explanations to his questions and concerns. Provide calming activities that you can do together. Help your child express himself and encourage him to find and trust his own voice. Remember to breathe, take your time, and reestablish family rituals and routines as soon as you can. I encourage you to seek out professionals who will support you and your child through this difficult time.

CONCLUDING THOUGHTS

In the remaining chapters you will find additional resources to help you on your journey, including a list of grief support groups and organizations, online resources, and a list of grief centers around the country. I've also included an annotated selection of books that you and your child many find useful.

I wrote this book to help you gather your strength so that you are able to communicate with your child now that you are sharing something as profound as the death of someone you both love. This is your task today and for a lifetime. I am honored to have walked with you for a time on your sacred journey.

∞ 18 ∞

Choosing a Grief Support Group

If you don't have a strong support network and would like to meet people who have had a similar experience to your own, or if you've attended a support group in the past and found it to be helpful, then a grief support group is worth trying out. A whole range of grief support groups are sponsored by hospices, hospitals, religious groups, and grief support centers.

There are four styles of bereavement support groups: drop-in groups, time-limited groups, ongoing groups, and self-help groups.

Drop-In Groups

Drop-in groups typically meet monthly or biweekly and usually require no registration ahead of time, or any commitment to return. The sessions are about two hours long and light refreshments are served. There may be a minimal fee to attend, but many are free of charge. Participants can keep returning to the group as often as they like, and the groups are facilitated either by

professional grief counselors or trained volunteers. Some participants are attracted to the informality of this type of group.

Time-Limited Groups

Time-limited groups meet weekly or biweekly, usually for six
to ten weeks. They require both preregistration and a commitment on the part of every participant to try to attend the entire
series. Professional grief counselors usually facilitate the meetings,
and typically there is a fee. Some people find time-limited groups
preferable to drop-in groups because the structure allows for
greater intimacy and safety.

Ongoing Groups

These require preregistration, but they are not as structured
as a time-limited series. Instead, participants choose on their
own how long they want to participate. The meetings are held
weekly, biweekly, or monthly; usually are facilitated by a bereavement professional; and usually require a fee. Some participants find that ongoing groups combine the safety and intimacy
of time-limited groups with the added flexibility of drop-in
groups.

Regardless of the format, what happens in the groups will
vary dramatically, so if you are considering attending a group, try
matching up your particular grief style with the group you choose.
For instance, traditional bereavement support groups cater to
feeling-focused grievers, and involve sitting together and sharing
feelings. While this works very well for many, if you find yourself

squirming in your chair during a group and counting the minutes until it ends, you might do better in a group that doesn't put a huge emphasis on sharing feelings. Action-oriented grievers usually fare much better in book discussion grief groups, journaling workshops, or hiking groups for the bereaved, because they tend to emphasize thinking and doing and not just feelings. If action-oriented groups aren't offered by your local hospice, church, or agency, ask for them. Of course, you may also prefer grieving more privately. Support groups are not for everyone.

Self-Help Groups

Typically, trained nonprofessionals facilitate self-help groups. Facilitators are usually bereaved themselves, but far enough along in their own grief to have the perspective needed to lead others. These are typically monthly drop-in groups, but as you'll discover, the format varies. Often, self-help groups are sponsored by nationwide or international organizations and they are designed to meet specialized needs of various bereavement populations.

The following list is not inclusive of all bereavement self-help groups, but it will give you an idea of the scope of these sorts of programs and help you access a broad range of self-help opportunities for you and your child.

ACCESS (Air Craft Casualty Emotional Support Services)

This is a national network for people who have lost a loved one in an aircraft-related tragedy. It matches the bereaved person with volunteers who have previously experienced a similar loss. It is exclusively an e-mail or telephone network.

Air Craft Casualty Emotional Support Services
1202 Lexington Avenue, Suite 335
New York, NY 10028
Phone: 877-227-6435
Website: http://www.accesshelp.org

American Association of Retired Persons (AARP)

AARP offers online bereavement support.
Website: http://www.aarp.org

American Association of Suicidology

This national organization offers resources for suicide prevention and the survivors of suicide (SOS). They provide a newsletter, a directory of resources for suicide prevention, conferences,
and referrals to local SOS chapters.

American Association of Suicidology
4201 Connecticut Avenue, NW, Suite 310
Washington, DC 20008
Phone: 202-237-2280
Website: http://www.suicidology.org

Autoerotic Asphyxiation Support

This online organization provides a supportive message board
for family and friends of those who have died by autoerotic as-
phyxiation.

Website: http://www.groups.yahoo.com/group/autoerotic
asphyxiationsupport

Bereaved Parents of the U.S.A.

This national support group for bereaved parents, siblings, and
grandparents offers a newsletter, referrals to local chapters, and
conferences.

Bereaved Parents of the U.S.A.
PO Box 95
Park Forest, IL 60466
Phone: 708-748-7672
Fax: 708-748-9184
Website: http://www.bereavedparents.org

Centre for Suicide Prevention

SIEC has extensive information on suicide prevention, postvention, and intervention efforts and trends. They offer a newsletter and referrals to local support services.

Suicide Information & Education Centre
1615-10th Avenue SW, Suite 201
Calgary, Alberta T3C 0J7
Canada
Phone: 403-245-3900
Website: http://www.suicideinfo.ca

The Compassionate Friends (TCF)

This is the largest self-help organization in the world for bereaved parents, siblings, and grandparents. They provide more than 650 local chapters in the United States and Canada, with national and regional conferences. TCF offers national and local newsletters, books and tapes, and other related bereavement resources.

The Compassionate Friends
PO Box 3696
Oak Brook, IL 60522-3696
Phone: 877-969-0010
Website: http://www.compassionatefriends.org

The Compassionate Friends of Canada

This is a volunteer self-help organization for parents grieving the death of a child of any age. They have over 130 local chapters and offer national and chapter newsletters.

The Compassionate Friends of Canada
#264270 Ponderosa Crescent
V8Z7H3
Canada
Phone: 866-823-0141
Website: http://www.tcfcanada.net

The Compassionate Friends of the U.K.

This nationwide organization of bereaved parents offers friendship and understanding to other bereaved parents, with affiliations around the world. They provide one-to-one and/or group support.

The Compassionate Friends
53 North Street
Bristol BS3 1EN
United Kingdom
Helpline: 0117 953 9639
Admin/fax: 0117 966 5202
Website: http://www.tcf.org.uk

COPS (Concerns of Police Survivors, Inc.)

This national organization provides resources for the surviving families of law enforcement officers killed in the line of duty. They sponsor an annual National Police Survivors' Conference each May during National Police Week, special hands-on programs for survivors, a summer camp for children (ages six to fourteen) and their parent/guardian, parents' retreats, spousal retreats, Outward Bound experiences for young adults (ages fifteen to twenty), a siblings retreat, and an adult children's and in-laws retreat.

Concerns of Police Survivors, Inc.
PO Box 3199
3096 South State Highway 5
Camdenton, MO 65020
Phone: 573-346-4911
Fax: 573-346-1414
Website: http://www.nationalcops.org

Delta Society

This online organization maintains a list of pet bereavement support groups, pet loss resource persons, counselors, and hotlines.
Delta Society
675 124th Avenue, Suite 101
Bellevue, WA 98055
Phone: 425-679-5500
Website: http://www.deltasociety.org

GriefShare

This national organization with 3,200 affiliated groups is a network of Christian support groups for the bereaved. It provides information and referrals, literature, and help in starting groups.
GriefShare
PO Box 1739
Wake Forest, NC 27588
Phone: 800-395-5755
Website: http://www.griefshare.org

Grieving Center

This is a Web-based television channel devoted to assisting those who have lost loved ones.
Website: http://www.grievingcenter.org

GROWW (Grief Recovery Online [founded by] Widows and Widowers

GROWW offers a large variety of volunteer-run bereavement chat rooms dealing with specific issues (e.g., loss of someone to drugs, a child, sibling, parent, loss due to long-term illness, sudden death, violent losses, gays and lesbians, men and many more).

Website: http://www.groww.org

Mothers Against Drunk Driving (MADD)

A national organization dedicated to stopping drunk driving and to supporting victims of this violent crime, MADD has over 500 local chapters and offers victim support groups for the bereaved. MADD has a newsletter, magazine, training programs, and conferences.

Mothers Against Drunk Driving
511 East John Carpenter Freeway, Suite 700
Irving, TX 75062
Phone: 800-GET-MADD
Website: http://www.madd.org

Mothers in Sympathy & Support (MISS)

MISS is a grassroots organization dedicated to supporting parents one-to-one after the death of an infant or young child.

The MISS Foundation
c/o Joanne Cacciatore, Founder
PO Box 5333
Peoria, AZ 85385-5333
Phone: 623-979-1000
Website: http://www.missfoundation.org

National Alliance for Grieving Children

This organization provides education and resources for anyone who wants to support grieving children.

Website: http://nationalalliance for grieving children.org

National Fallen Firefighters Foundation
Survivors Support Network

This national organization provides emotional support to spouses, families, and friends of firefighters who have died in the line of duty. Members are matched with survivors of similar experiences to help them cope during the difficult months following the death.

National Fallen Firefighters Foundation
PO Drawer 498
Emmitsburg, MD 21727
Phone: 301-447-1365
Website: http://www.firehero.org

National Hospice and Palliative Care Organization (NHPCO)

NHPCO offers referrals to more than 2,100 hospices, a national newsletter, magazine, volunteer and professional conferences, and related support resources.

National Hospice and Palliative Care Organization
1700 Diagonal Road, Suite 625
Alexandria, VA 22314
Phone: 800-658-8898
Website: http://www.nhpco.org

National Students of Ailing Mothers and Fathers
Support Network (AMF)

AMF is a network of university students helping each other cope with the serious illness or death of a parent or loved one.

They are actively developing campus-based mutual support groups around the United States and also offer an online newsletter, online chats, and service projects. Their website provides information, group development guidelines, and a listing of universities currently developing support groups.

National Students of AMF
514 Daniels Street, Suite 356
Raleigh, NC 27605
Website: http://www.studentsofamf.org

Parents of Murdered Children (POMC)

This is the largest self-help organization in the world for parents, families, friends, and other victims of homicide. POMC has more than 400 local chapters and contact persons in the United States and abroad. In addition to groups, they provide newsletters and offer conferences.

Parents of Murdered Children
100 East 8th Street, Suite 202
Cincinnati, OH 45202
Phone: 513-721-5683
Website: http://www.pomc.org

Pet Loss Grief Support Website

This moderated board offers support and understanding for persons grieving the loss of their pet or who have a pet that is ill. It also offers Monday Pet Loss Candle Ceremony, a chat room, tribute pages, and other resources.

Website: http://www.petloss.com

Rainbows

This is an international organization with 8,600 affiliated groups, offering peer support groups in churches, schools, or social agencies for children and adults who are grieving a death, divorce, or other painful transition in their family.

Rainbows
2100 Golf Road, Suite 370
Rolling Meadows, IL 60008-4231
Phone: 800-266-3206 or 847-952-1770
Fax: 847-952-1774
Website: http://www.rainbows.org

SIDS Alliance

This is a national organization supporting families who have suffered sudden infant death syndrome. SIDS Alliance has more than 50 local chapters and offers a newsletter and conferences.

SIDS Alliance
1314 Bedford Avenue, Suite 210
Baltimore, MD 21208
Phone: 800-221-SIDS
Website: http://www.firstcandle.org

TAPS (Tragedy Assistance Program for Survivors)

This is a national network providing support for persons who have lost a loved one while serving in the armed forces (Army, Air Force, Navy, Marine Corps, National Guard, Reserves, Service Academies, Coast Guard, and contractors serving beside the military). TAPS offers networking, crisis information, problem-solving assistance and liaison with military agencies. There are also extensive TAPS youth programs and an annual multigenerational gathering in Washington, DC.

Tragedy Assistance Program for Survivors
910 17th Street NW, Suite 800
Washington, DC 20006

Phone: 800-959-8277
Website: http://www.taps.org

Twinless Twin Support Group

This is an international support network that provides mutual support for twins and other multiples who have lost their twin or multiple(s).

Twinless Twin Support Group
PO Box 980481
Ypsilanti, MI 48198
Phone: 888-205-8962
Website: http://www.twinlesstwins.org
E-mail: contact@twinlesstwins.org

Wings of Light, Inc.

This national organization provides support and information to individuals affected by aviation accidents. It provides separate networks for airplane accident survivors, families and friends of persons killed in airplane accidents, and persons involved in rescue, recovery, and investigation of crashes.

Wings of Light, Inc.
PMB 448, 16845 North 29th Avenue, Suite 1
Phoenix, AZ 85053
Voice: 623-516-1115
Website: http://www.wingsoflight.org

∞ 19 ∞

Finding a Grief Support Center

The best example of a family-focused grief support center is the Dougy Center in Portland, Oregon. It was the first of its kind in the United States to provide peer support groups for grieving children. Since 1982, it has offered a safe place for over twenty thousand grieving children, teens, young adults, and their families. The Dougy Center operates on a facilitated peer-support model and is not therapy, although it does offer a therapy referral list to families. It is a nonprofit organization, and there is never a fee for services at the Dougy Center.

Its groups are open to children, teens, and young adults who have experienced the death of a parent, primary caregiver, sibling, or, in the case of teens, a close friend. The young adult group is open to people between the ages of nineteen and thirty who have experienced any significant death. All participants gather every other week, along with trained group facilitators. Groups are one and a half hours long and organized according to age groups and the cause of death. Age groups are as follows: children three to five, children six to twelve, children eleven to fourteen, teens thirteen to eighteen, and young adults nineteen to thirty.

The Dougy Center groups offer a range of opportunities to participants, including talking about the death, using an art room, playing in a dramatic playroom, or venting big feelings in a safe, "padded" room. Parents or guardians meet together for information and support at the same time as the young people are meeting.

Due to its tremendous success, the Dougy Center has been replicated all across the country, and in several countries outside the United States. To find a grief support center near where you live, refer to the statewide listing below. The organizations with an asterisk were trained in the Dougy Center model.

Alabama
Hospice of Marshall Co., Inc.
8787 US Highway 431
Albertville, AL 35950
256-891-7724
888-334-9336 toll-free
http://www.hospicemc.org

Hospice of EAMC
665 Opelika Road
Auburn, AL 36830
334-826-1899
334-826-0756 fax

* Amelia Center
1513 4th Avenue S
Birmingham, AL 35233
205-251-3430
205-251-5146 fax
http://www.ameliacenter.org

* Hospice of Cullman County
402 4th Avenue NE
Cullman, AL 35055
256-739-5185
256-737-0985 fax

* Healing House Community
   Bereavement Center
240 Johnston Street SE
Decatur, AL 35602
256-350-5585
http://www.hospiceofthevalley.net

Wiregrass Hospice Inc.
2740 Headland Avenue
Dothan, AL 36303
334-792-1100
800-626-1101 toll-free
334-794-0009 fax
http://www.wiregrasshospice.org

The Caring House
Hospice Family Care
3304 Westmill Drive
Huntsville, AL 35805
256-650-1212
888-619-8000 toll-free
256-880-2929 fax
http://www.hospicefamilycare.org

Healing Place and Hospice of the
   Shoals:
A Partnership of Compassion
5604 Ricks Lane
Tuscumbia, AL 35674-5925
256-383-7133
256-383-7996 fax
http://www.thehealingplaceinfo
   .org

Alaska
* Forget Me Not Grief Program
500 West International Airport
   Road, Suite C
Anchorage, AK 99518
907-338-4727
907-561-0334 fax
http://www.hospiceofanchorage.org

Arizona
Hospice of the Valley
Grief Speak
1510 East Flowers Street
Phoenix, AZ 85014
602-530-6987
http://www.hospiceofthevalley.org

* New Song Center for Grieving
   Children
6947 East McDonald Drive
Scottsdale, AZ 85253
480-951-8985
480-951-8794 fax
http://www.thenewsongcenter.org

* Tu Nidito Children and Family
   Services
3922 North Mountain Avenue
Tucson, AZ 85719-1313
520-322-9155
520-321-0831 fax
http://www.tunidito.org

Arkansas

Center for Good Mourning
Arkansas Children's Hospital
800 Marshall Street, Slot 669
Little Rock, AR 72202
501-364-7000
501-364-5230 fax
http://www.archildrens.org/
   community_outreach/cent

* Kaleidoscope Kids
1501 North University Avenue,
   Suite 680
Little Rock, AR 72207
501-978-5437
877-357-5437 toll-free
501-537-2718 fax
http://www.kaleidoscopekids.org

California
* Greater Hope Foundation for
   Children
231 East Main Street
Barstow, CA 92311
760-256-0432
760-256-0537 fax
http://homepage.mac.com/
   gdandscompserv/home01.htm

* Hospice of the North Coast
   Community Outreach
5441 Avenida Encinas, Suite A
Carlsbad, CA 92008

760-431-4100
760-431-4133 fax
http://www.hospicenorthcoast.org

Comfort for Kids
2051 Harrison Street
Concord, CA 94520
925-609-1830
925-609-1841 fax
http://www.hospicecc.org

Hospice of Marin Youth Bereavement Program
150 Nellen Avenue
Corte Madera, CA 94925
415-927-2273
415-927-2284 fax
http://www.hospiceofmarin.org

Yolo Hospice
PO Box 1014
Davis, CA 95617
530-758-5648
800-491-7711 toll-free
530-758-5122 fax
http://www.yolohospice.org

* Hope Hospice
6500 Dublin Boulevard, Suite 100
Dublin, CA 94568
925-829-8770
925-829-0868 fax
http://www.hopehospice.com

Elizabeth Hospice
150 West Crest Street
Escondido, CA 92025
760-737-2050
760-796-3788 fax
http://www.elizabethhospice.org

Footsteps at Saint Agnes Medical
   Center
1303 East Herndon
Fresno, CA 93720
559-450-5608
http://www.samc.com

Hinds Hospice Center for Grief
   & Loss
Angel Babies & Bereavement
1616 West Shaw, B-6
Fresno, CA 93711
559-248-8579
http://www.hindshospice.org

Center for Grief and Loss
1010 North Central
Glendale, CA 91202

866-74GRIEF (866-744-7433)
   toll-free
818-249-3864 fax
http://www.griefcenterforchildren
   .org

Griefbusters of Amador
Hospice of Amador
PO Box 595
Jackson, CA 95642
209-223-5500
209-223-4964 fax

* Gary's Place for Kids
23332 Mill Creek Drive,
   Suite 230
Laguna Hills, CA 92653
949-348-0548
949-770-4688 fax
http://www.gpfkoc.org

Wings of Hope
Hospice Services of Lake County
1717 South Main Street
Lakeport, CA 95453
707-263-6222
http://www.hospice-lakecountyca
   .org

Camp Hope
5535 Arroyo Road
Livermore, CA 94550
619-594-4389
http://www.camphopeca.com

Pathways Volunteer Hospice:
  Changes
3300 East South Street, Suite 206
Long Beach, CA 90805
562-531-3031
562-531-3037 fax
http://www.pathwayshospice.org

Center for Grief and Loss
924 West 70th Street
Los Angeles, CA 90044
866-74GRIEF
213-924-3510
818-249-3864 fax
http://www.griefcenterforchildren
  .org

* Our House—A Grief Support
  Center
1950 Sawtelle Boulevard, Suite
  255
Los Angeles, CA 90025
310-475-0299
310-475-2985 fax
http://www.ourhouse-grief.org

Community Hospice, Inc.
601 McHenry Avenue
Modesto, CA 95350
209-578-6300
209-577-0738 fax
http://www.hospiceheart.org

* Good Grief for Kids
Community Hospital of the Monterey Peninsula
23625 Holman Highway
Monterey, CA 93942
831-625-4753
http://www.chomp.org

* Drew's Place
138 New Mohawk, Suite 6
Nevada City, CA 95959
530-265-0341
503-265-0719 fax

Circle of Care
2540 Charleston Street
Oakland, CA 94602
510-531-7551
510-531-3657 fax
http://www.ebac.org/programs

* Mourning Star Center
42-600 Cook Street, Suite 202
Palm Desert, CA 92211
760-836-0360
760-776-1612 fax
http://www.mourningstar.org/

KARA Grief Support
457 Kingsley Avenue
Palo Alto, CA 94301
650-321-5272
650-473-1828 fax
http://www.kara-grief.org

Center for Grief and Loss
37 North Holliston
Pasadena, CA 91106
866-74GRIEF (866-744-7433)
   toll-free
818-249-3864 fax
http://www.griefcenterforchildren
   .org

Hospice of Petaluma/Children
   and Teen Program
416 Payran Street
Petaluma, CA 94952
707-778-6242
707-778-0144 fax

Gathering Place
514 North Prospect, Suite 115
Redondo Beach, CA 90277
310-374-6323
310-374-6595 fax
http://www.griefcenter.info/
   welcome.html

Children's Bereavement Art
   Group
2800 L Street, Suite 400
Sacramento, CA 95816
916-454-6555
916-454-6526 fax

Griefbusters/Hospice of the Central Coast
945 S Main Street, Suite 101
Salinas, CA 93901
831-649-7755
831-753-0402 fax
http://www.chomp.org

Sharp Hospice Care
4000 Ruffin Road, Suite A
San Diego, CA 92123
619-667-1900
619-667-1950 fax
http://www.sharp.com

* Josie's Place for Bereaved Youth
and Families
3288 21st Street, Suite 139 (mailing address)
San Francisco, CA 94110
415-513-6343

George Mark Children's House
2121 George Mark Lane
San Leandro, CA 94578
510-346-4624
510-346-4620 fax
http://www.georgemark.org

Hospice of San Luis Opispo
County, Inc.
1304 Pacific Street
San Luis Opisbo, CA 93401
805-544-2266
805-544-6573 fax
http://www.hospiceslo.org

Centre for Living with Dying
1265 El Camino Real, Suite 208
Santa Clara, CA 95050
408-553-6950
http://www.thecentre.org

Touchstone Support Network
3041 Olcott Street
Santa Clara, CA 95054-3222

408-727-5775
408-727-0182 fax
http://www.php.com

Sutter VNA and Hospice Children's Services
1110 North Dutton Avenue
Santa Rosa, CA 95401
707-535-5780
http://www.suttervnaandhospice
.org

International Network for Attitudinal Healing
33 Buchanan Drive
Sausalito, CA 94965
415-331-6161
415-331-4545 fax
http://www.attitudinalhealing.org

Grief Recovery Institute
PO Box 6061-382
Sherman Oaks, CA 91413
818-907-9600
818-907-9329 fax
http://www.grief-recovery.com

* Willmar Center for Bereaved
  Children
PO Box 1374
Sonoma, CA 95476
707-935-1946
707-935-1770 fax

* Dawn's Light: A Center for
  Children and Adults in Grief
PO Box 4733
591 South Washington Street,
  Suite B
Sonora, CA 95370
209-532-9001
http://www.dawnslight.org

* Mourning Star Center
12421 Hesperia Road, Suite 11
Victorville, CA 92345
760-241-3564, ext. 250
760-241-6885 fax
http://www.mourningstar.org

Contra Costa Crisis Center
PO Box 3364
Walnut Creek, CA 94598
925-939-1916
(925-944-0645) 24-hour toll-free
925-939-1933 fax
http://www.crisis-center.org

Our House—A Grief Support
  Center
21860 Burbank Boulevard
Woodland Hills, CA 91367
818-222-3344
www.ourhouse-grief.org

Colorado
* Healing Circles
HospiceCare Grief and Education
  Center
1585 Patton Drive
Boulder, CO 80303
303-604-5330
303-604-5350 fax
http://www.hospicecareonline.org

* Hospice of Metro Denver
The Footprints Grief Center
501 South Cherry Street,
  Suite 700
Denver, CO 80246-1234
303-321-2828
303-321-7171 fax
http://www.hmd.org

* Judi's House
The Judith Ann Griese Founda-
    tion
1741 Gaylord Street
Denver, CO 80206
720-941-0331
720-941-0728 fax
http://www.judishouse.org

* The Lighthouse
2379 South High Street
Denver, CO 80210
303-722-2319
877-722-2319 toll-free
http://www.childgrief.org/
    lighthouse.htm

Mt. Evans Hospice
Camp Comfort
3081 Bergen Peak Drive
Evergreen, CO 80439
303-674-6400
303-674-8813 fax
http://www.campcomfort.org

Center for Loss and Life Transi-
    tion
3735 Broken Bow Road
Fort Collins, CO 80526
970-226-6050
970-226-6051 fax
http://www.centerforloss.com

Hospice and Palliative Care of
    Western Colorado
Child and Teen Center
2754 Compass Drive, Suite 377
Grand Junction, CO 81506
970-241-2212
970-257-2400 fax
http://www.gvhospice.com

Sangre De Cristo Hospice & Pal-
    liative Care
1107 Pueblo Boulevard Way
Pueblo, CO 81005
719-542-0032
719-542-1413 fax

The Dragonfly Program: Grief
    Support Program for Young
    People
Exempla Lutheran Hospice at
    Collier Hospice Center
3210 Lutheran Parkway
Wheat Ridge, CO 80033
303-403-7274
303-403-7295 fax
http://www.exempla.org/body.cfm
    ?id=468

Connecticut

* Healing Hearts Center for
  Grieving Children & Families
72 Stadley Rough Road
Danbury, CT 06810-4710
203-792-4422
203-739-8301
http://www.regionalhospicct.org/
  healing_hearts.htm

* Center for Hope, Inc.
590 Post Road
Darien, CT 06820
203-655-0547
203-972-0556 fax
http://www.centerforhope.org

* Den for Grieving Kids/Family
  Centers, Inc.
40 Arch Street
Greenwich, CT 06830
203-869-4848
203-869-7764 fax
http://www.centerforhope.org

Cove Center for Grieving
  Children
134 State Street
Meriden, CT 06450
203-634-0500

800-750-COVE (800-750-2683)
  toll-free
203-634-6934 fax
http://www.covect.org

Cove/West Hartford
854 Farmington Avenue
West Hartford, CT 06119
860-233-1700

Mary's Place/A Center for Grieving Children & Families
6 Poquonock Avenue
Windsor, CT 06095-2507
860-688-9621
860-683-0206 fax
http://www.marysplacect.com

Delaware
Delaware Hospice
600 DuPont Highway, Suite 107
Georgetown, DE 19947
302-856-7717
800-838-9800 toll-free
302-479-2586 fax
http://www.delawarehospice.org

* Supporting Kidds/A Center for
   Grieving Children & Families
1213 Old Lancaster Pike
Hockessin, DE 19707
302-235-5544
302-235-2672 fax
http://www.supportingkidds.org

Washington, DC
Wendt Center for Loss and
   Healing
4201 Connecticut Avenue NW,
   Suite 300
Washington, D.C. 20008
202 624 0010
202-624-0062 fax
http://www.wendtcenter.org

Florida
Bethany Center for Grieving
   Children
105 Arneson Avenue
Auburndale, FL 33823
863-968-1707
http://www.goodshepherdhospice
   .org/

Hospice of Citrus County
PO Box 641270
Beverly Hills, FL 34464

352-527-2020
352-527-0386 fax
http://www.hospiceofcitruscounty
   .org

Hospice by the Sea, Inc.
1531 West Palmetto Park Road
Boca Raton, FL 33486-3395
561-395-5031
561-393-7137 fax
http://www.hospicebytheseafl.org

* Tomorrow's Rainbow
4341 Northwest 39th Avenue
Coconut Creek, FL 33073
954-978-2390
http://www.tomorrowsrainbow.org

Begin Again Children's Grief
   Center
655 North Clyde Morris Boulevard, Suite A
Daytona Beach, FL 32114
386-258-5100
386-258-9889 fax

* Begin Again Children's Grief
  Center
1250 South Spring Garden Avenue, Suite 3
Deland, FL 32720
386-822-4852

* Hope Hospice Rainbow Center
9470 HealthPark Circle
Fort Myers, FL 33908
239-482-4673
800-835-1673 toll-free
941-482-7298 fax
http://www.hopehospice.org

Community Hospice of Northeast
  Florida
Grief and Loss Center
4266 Sunbeam Road
Jacksonville, FL 03257
904-268-5200
904-596-6110 fax

* Suncoast Kid's Place
17030 Lakeshore Road
Lutz, FL 33558
813-990-0216
813-960-1091 fax
http://www.suncoastkidsplace.org

* New Hope for Kids
900 North Maitland Avenue
Maitland, FL 32751
407-599-0909
407-599-0904 fax
http://www.newhopeforkids.org

* Bright Star Center for Grieving
  Children
Hospice of Health First
300 East New Haven Avenue
Melbourne, FL 32901
321-733-7672
321-733-2741 fax

Catholic Hospice
14875 N.W. 77 Avenue,
  Suite 100
Miami Lakes, FL 33016
305-822-2380
305-824-0665 fax
http://www.catholichospice.org

Bereavement Center New Port
  Richey
Gulfside Regional Hospice
6224 Lafayette Street
New Port Richey, FL 34652
727-844-3946
http://www
  .gulfsideregionalhospice.org

Hospice of the Emerald Coast
2925 MLK Boulevard
Panama City, FL 32405
850-769-0055
877-717-7357 toll-free
http://www.hospiceemeraldcoast
.org

* Children's Bereavement Center
7600 South Red Road, Suite 307
South Miami, FL 33143
305-668-4902
305-669-9110 fax
http://www.childbereavement.org

The Caring Tree of Big Bend
Hospice
1723 Mahan Center Boulevard
Tallahassee, FL 32308
850-878-5310
850-309-1639 fax
http://www.bigbendhospice.org

Lee's Place, Inc.
216 Lake Ella Drive
Tallahassee, FL 32303
850-841-7733
850-841-7702 fax
http://www.leesplace.org

* Circle of Love Center for
  Grieving Children
LifePath Hospice & Palliative
  Care, Inc.
3010 West Azeele Street
Tampa, FL 33609
813-877-2200
800-209-2200 toll-free
813-872-7037 fax
http://www.lifepath-hospice.org/
  patients/center.html

Kathy's Place 4 Hope
730 South Sterling Avenue
Tampa, FL 33609
813-875-0728
http://www.aplace4hope.org

Hospice of Lake Sumter, Inc.
2445 Lane Park Road
Tavares, FL 32778
352-343-1341
352-343-6115 fax
http://www.hospicels.com

* Hospice of St. Francis
North Star Program
1250-B Grumman Place
Titusville, FL 32780
321-264-1687
321-269-5428 fax
http://www.hospiceofstfrancis
  .com

* Bright Star Center for Grieving
  Children
1900 Dairy Road
West Melbourne, FL 32904
321-733-7672

Hearts and Hope, Inc.
317 10th Street
West Palm Beach, FL 33401
561-832-1913
561-832-1947 fax
http://www.heartsandhope.org

* Horizons Bereavement Center
Hospice of Palm Beach County
5300 East Avenue
West Palm Beach, FL 33407
561-227-5175 (Horizons)
561-848-5200 (hospice) toll-free
http://www.hpbc.com

Georgia
* House Next Door
348 Mount Vernon Highway NE
Atlanta, GA 30328
404-256-9797
404-256-3483 fax
http://www.thelink.org

Rising Sun Center for Loss and
  Renewal
2848 Windsor Oaks Trace
Marietta, GA 30066
770-928-1027
770-592-4428 fax
http://www.risingsuncenter.com

Hope for Grieving Children
Roswell First Baptist Church
710 Mimosa Boulevard
Roswell, GA 30075
770-915-2537
770-587-6990 fax

Full Circle Grief & Loss Center
Hospice of Savannah
PO Box 13190
Savannah, GA 31406
912-355-2289
888-355-4911 toll-free
912-355-2376 fax
http://www.hospicesavannah.org

Hawaii

Hospice Hawaii
860 Iwilei Road
Honolulu, HI 96817-5018
808-924-9255
808-922-9161 fax
http://www.hospicehawaii.org

* Kids Hurt Too
PO Box 11260
Honolulu, HI 96828
808-735-2989
808-735-2989 fax
http://www.grievingyouth.org

* Queen Lili'uokalani Children's
   Center
4530 Kali Road
Koloa, HI 96766
808-245-1873
808-245-2167 fax

* Kauai Hospice
Forget Me Not
PO Box 3286
Lihue, HI 96766
808-245-7277
808-245-5006 fax
http://www.kauaihospice.org

Idaho

* Touchstone, Center for Grieving Children
3800 East Shady Glen
Boise, ID 83706
208-377-3216
http://www.touchstonecenter.org

* Hospice of North Idaho
9493 North Government Way
Hayden, ID 83835
208-772-7994
208-772-5916 fax

Willow Center
PO Box 1361
Lewiston, ID 83501
509-780-1156

Bonner Community Hospice
PO Box 1448
Sandpoint, ID 83864
208-265-1179
208-265-1085 fax
http://www.bonnergen.org

Kids Count Too!
826 Eastland Drive
Twin Falls, ID 83301
208-734-4061
800-540-4061 toll-free
208-734-3471 fax

Illinois

Hospice of Northeastern Illinois
410 South Hager Avenue
Barrington, IL 60010
847-381-5599, ext. 214
847-381-8042 fax
http://www.hospiceanswers.org

Kid's Time Grief Support Group
St. Elizabeth's Hospital
211 South 3rd Street
Belleville, IL 62222-1998
618-234-2120
618-222-4650 fax

Adventist St. Thomas Hospice
8230 South Madison Street
Burr Ridge, IL 60527
630-856-6990
630-856-6999 fax

Center for Grief Recovery
Institute for Creativity
1263 West Loyola, Suite 100
Chicago, IL 60626
773-274-4600
http://www.griefcounselor.org

Companionship Bereavement
  Program
5721 South Maryland Avenue,
  K111C
University of Chicago
Chicago, IL 60637
773-834-1776
773-702-5440 fax

* Heartlight
Children's Memorial Hospital
2300 Children's Plaza
Chicago, IL 60614-3363
773-975-8829
773-880-4974 fax
http://www.childrensmemorial.org

Kids Clubhouse
Five 157 Center
Edwardsville, IL 62025
618-656-1600

* Heart Connection
Pastoral Care Department
2800 West 95th Street
Evergreen Park, IL 60805
708-229-5480
708-422-2212 fax

Fox Valley Hospice & Care for
the Bereaved
Herbie's Friends
200 Whitfield Drive
Geneva, IL 60134
630-232-2233
630-232-0023 fax
http://www.foxvalleyhospice.net

Midwest Palliative & Hospice
Care Center
2050 Claire Court
Glenview, IL 60025
800-331-5484 toll-free
847-556-1611 fax
http://www.carecenter.org

Willow House
3330 Dundee Road, Suite S1-S4
Northbrook, IL 60062
847-205-5666
847-205-5665 fax
http://www.willowhouse.org

Rainbows, Inc. International
2100 Golf Road, Unit 370
Rolling Meadows, IL 60008-4231
847-952-1770
800-266-3206 toll-free
847-952-1774 fax
http://www.rainbows.org

Buddy's Place
1023 West Burlington Avenue
Western Springs, IL 60558
708-354-5280
708-354-0867 fax

Indiana
* Erin's House for Grieving Children, Inc.
3811 Illinois Road, Suite 205
Parkwest Center & Administration
Fort Wayne, IN 46804
260-423-2466
260-423-4584 fax
http://www.erinshouse.org

* Ryan's Place
PO Box 73
Goshen, IN 46527
574-535-1000
http://www.ryans-place.org

Brooke's Place for Grieving
Young People, Inc.
50 East 91st Street, Suite 103
Indianapolis, IN 46240
317-705-9650
317-705-9654 fax
http://www.brookesplace.org

Mending Hearts
Boys and Girls Clubs of Wayne
    County
1717 South L Street
Richmond, IN 47374
765-962-6922
765-939-6273 fax
http://www.bgcrichmond.org

Iowa

Rick's House of Hope for Griev-
    ing & Traumatized Children
Genesis Medical Center
1227 East Rusholme Street
Davenport, IA 52803
563-324-9580
563-324-9580 fax
http://www.genesishealth.com

Amanda the Panda
1000 73rd Street, Suite 12
Des Moines, IA 50311
515-223-4847
515-223-4782 fax
http://www.amandathepanda.org

Hospice of Siouxland
4300 Hamilton Boulevard
Sioux City, IA 51104-1100
712-233-4100
800-383-4545 toll-free

Eucalyptus Tree Program
Cedar Valley Hospice
PO Box 2880
Waterloo, IA 50704-2880
319-272-2002
800-617-1972 toll-free
319-272-2071 fax
http://www.cvhospice.org

Kansas

* Guidance Center
500 Limit Street
Leavenworth, KS 66048
913-682-5118
913-682-4664 fax

* Solace House
8012 State Line Road, Suite 202
Shawnee Mission, KS 66208
913-341-0318
913-341-0319 fax
http://www.solacehouse.org

Three Trees Center
8100 East 22nd Street N
Building 800, Suite 100
Wichita, KS 67226
316-263-3335
http://www.threetrees.org

Kentucky
RENEW: Center for Personal
Recovery
201 Overland Ridge, Suite 157
Walton, KY 41094
513-376-9954
http://www.renew.net

Stars Program
Gloria Dei Lutheran Church
2718 Dixie Highway
Crestview Hills, KY 41017
859-292-0244
http://www.starsforchildren.com

Hospice & Palliative Care of
Central Kentucky
105 Diecks Drive
PO Box 2149
Elizabethtown, KY 42702
270-737-6300
800-686-9577 toll-free
270-737-4053 fax

Hospice of the Bluegrass
2312 Alexandria Drive
Lexington, KY 40504-3277
859-276-5344
800-876-6005 toll-free
859-223-0490 fax
http://www.hospicebg.com

The Hosparus Grief Counseling
Center
2120 Newburg Road, Suite 200
Louisville, KY 40205
502-456-5451
888-345-8197 toll-free
502-456-9701 fax
http://www.hospices.org/bridges
.htm

Louisiana
Project SKY/Grief Recovery
Center
4919 Jamestown Avenue,
Suite 102
Baton Rouge, LA 70808
225-924-6621
225-924-6627 fax

* Healing House
PO Box 3861
Lafayette, LA 70502
337-234-0443
http://www.healing-house.org

Seasons Grief Center
654 Brockenbraugh Court
Metairie, LA 70005
504-834-5957
504-834-1453 fax
http://www.seasonsgriefcenter.org

Maine

* Pathfinders: Hospice of Eastern
   Maine
EMHS Healthcare
885 Union Street, Suite 220
Bangor, ME 04401
207-973-8269
800-350-8269 toll-free
207-973-6557 fax
http://www.pathfindersmaine.org

Hospice Volunteers Center for
   Grief and Loss
45 Baribeau Drive
Brunswick, ME 04011
207-721-9702
888-486-0340 toll-free
http://www.hospicevolunteers.org

Grieving Children's Program
Hospice Volunteers of Kennebec
   Valley
150 Dresden Avenue
Gardiner, ME 04345
207-626-1779
207-582-6819 fax
http://www
   .hospicevolunteerskennebec
   .org

Program for Grieving Children
   & Teens
Androscoggin Home Care
   & Hospice
15 Strawberry Avenue
Lewiston, ME 04243-0819
207-777-7740
800-482-7412 toll-free
207-777-7748 fax

* The Center for Grieving
   Children
555 Forest Avenue
Portland, ME 04101
207-775-5216
207-773-7417 fax
http://www.cgcmaine.org

Hospice Volunteers of Waterville
   Area
Camp Ray of Hope
304 Main Street
Waterville, ME 04903
207-873-3615
207-873-5094 fax
http://www.hvwa.org

Maryland
Hospice of the Chesapeake
445 Defense Highway
Annapolis, MD 21401
410-987-2003
800-745-6132 toll-free
443-837-1505 fax
http://www.hospicechesapeake
 .org

Hospice of Frederick County
PO Box 1799
Frederick, MD 21702
240-566-3030
http://www.hospiceoffrederick.org

* Hospice of Charles County, Inc.
105 La Grange Avenue
PO Box 1703
La Plata, MD 20646
301-934-1268
888-934-1268 toll-free
301-934-3910 fax

* Calvert Hospice
238 Merrimac Court
Prince Frederick, MD 20678
410-535-0892
http://www.calverthospice.org

Montgomery Hospice
1355 Piccard Drive, Suite 100
Rockville, MD 20850
301-921-4400
301-921-4433 fax
http://www.montgomeryhospice
 .org

Me Too! / Stella Maris, Inc.
2300 Dulaney Valley Road
Timonium, MD 21093
410-252-4500

Carroll Hospice
Healing Hearts Support Group
292 Stoner Avenue
Westminster, MD 21157
410-871-7231
http://www.carrollhospice.org

Massachusetts
* Children's Room
1210 Massachusetts Avenue
Arlington, MA 02476
781-641-4741
781-641-0012 fax
http://www.childrensroom.org/

Good Grief Program
Boston Medical Center
One Boston Medical Center
    Place, 5th Floor
Boston, MA 02118
617-414-4005
http://www.goodgriefprogram.org

Hospice of the North Shore
75 Sylvan Street, Suite B-102
Danvers, MA 01923
978-774-7566
978-774-4389 fax
http://www.hns.org

* Children's Room
39 Edwards Street
Framingham, MA 01701
781-641-4741
781-641-0012 fax
http://www.childrensroom.org/

Merrimack Valley Hospice
360 Merrimack Street, Building 9
Lawrence, MA 01843
800-933-5593 toll-free
978-552-4001 fax
http://www
    .merrimackvalleyhospice.org

The Garden: A Center for
    Grieving Children & Teens
286 Prospect Street
Northampton, MA 01060
413-584-7086, ext. 124
http://www.garden-cgc.org

* Cranberry Hospice of CURA
    VNA
36 Cordage Park Circle,
    Suite 236
Plymouth, MA 02360
508-746-0215
508-830-3336 fax

HEART *play*
Parmenter VNA & Community
    Care
266 Cochituate Road
Wayland, MA 01778
508-358-3000
508-358-3005 fax
http://www.parmenter.org

The Human Relations Service
11 Chapel Place
Wellesley, MA 02481
781-235-4950
781-235-7176 fax

* Children's Friend
20 Cedar Street
Worcester, MA 01609
508-753-5425
508-757-7659 fax
http://www.childrensfriend.org

Michigan
Hospice of Lenawee
415 Mill Road
Adrian, MI 49221
517-263-2323
800-578-6559 toll-free
517-263-1279 fax

ᴵᴵᴵ Pathfinders: Grief Support for
   Children
Arbor Hospice
Grief Support Services
2366 Oak Valley Drive
Ann Arbor, MI 48103
734-662-5999
888-992-CARE (888-992-2273)
   toll-free
734-662-9000 fax
http://www.arborhospice.org

For the Kids Foundation
219 Elm Street
Birmingham, MI 48009-6306

888-987-5437 toll-free
248-642-3601 fax
http://www.forthekidsfoundation
   .org/

SandCastles Grief Support
   Program
Clinton Township, MI 48036
313-874-6881
http://www.aboutsandcastles.org

Open Arms Grief Support
4777 East Outer Drive, Suite
   G-500
Detroit, MI 48234
313-369-5780
313-369-5779
http://www.stjohn.org/openarms

SandCastles Grief Support
   Program
1 Ford Place, Suite 1B
Detroit, MI 48202-3450
313-874-6881
http://www.aboutsandcastles.org

Ele's Place
1145 West Oakland Avenue
Lansing, MI 48915
517-482-1315
517-482-6608 fax
http://www.elesplace.org

SandCastles Grief Support
    Program
Livonia, MI 48150
313-874-6881
http://www.aboutsandcastles.org

Mercy Memorial Hospice
    of Monroe
725 Monroe Street
Monroe, MI 48162
734-240-8940
734-240-8950 fax
http://www.mercymemorial.org

New Hope Center for Grief
    Support
New Hope for KIDZ & TEENS
113 East Dunlap
Northville, MI 48167
248-348-0115
248-348-6815 fax
http://www.newhopecenter.net

SandCastles Grief Support
    Program
St. Clair Shores, MI 48082
313-874-6881
http://www.aboutsandcastles.org

* Lory's Place
A Grief Healing and Education
    Center of Hospice at Home Inc.
445 Upton Drive, Suite 9
Saint Joseph, MI 49085
269-983-2707
800-717-3812 toll-free
269-983-2740 fax
http://www.lorysplace.org

SandCastles Grief Support
    Program
Southfield, MI 48076
313-874-6881
http://www.aboutsandcastles.org

Minnesota
Minnesota Valley Youth Grief
    Services
Fairview Ridges Hospital
201 East Nicollette Boulevard
Burnsville, MN 55337
952-892-2111
952-892-2466 fax

St. Mary's Grief Support Center
St Mary's Medical Center
407 East Third Street
Duluth, MN 55805
218-786-4402
218-786-4067 fax

The Healing Quilt
Children's Health Care
2525 Chicago Avenue South
Minneapolis, MN 55404
612-813-6622
612-813-6147 fax
http://www.childrenshc.org

* Katlin's Gift
5184 3rd Street NW
Rochester, MN 55901
507-282-7932
http://www.katlinsgift.org

Mississippi
* McClean Fletcher Center
2624 Southerland Street
Jackson, MS 39216
601-982-4406
601-982-4440 fax

Missouri
* Lost and Found: A Place for
   Hope and Grief
1006 Cedarbrook Avenue
Springfield, MO 65802
417-865-9998
417-832-9423 fax
http://www.lostandfoundozarks
   .com

Annie's Hope—The Bereave-
   ment Center for Kids
1333 West Lockwood, Suite 104
St. Louis, MO 63122
314-965-5015
314-918-1438 fax
http://www.annieshope.org

* Missouri Baptist Medical
   Center
Grief Support Program
3015 North Ballas Road
St. Louis, MO 63131
314-997-5057
314-996-5958 fax
http://www
   .missouribaptistmedicalcenter
   .org

Montana
Big Sky Hospice
The Bereavement Center
711 Central Avenue
Billings, MT 59101
406-247-3300
406-247-3303 fax

* Peace Hospice of Montana
Children's Bereavement Services
1101 26th Street South
Great Falls, MT 59405
406-455-3040

Tamarack Grief Resource Center
336 West Spruce Street
Missoula, MT 59802
406-721-2860

Nebraska
Charlie Brown's Kids—Good
   Grief
PO Box 67106
Lincoln, NE 68506
402-483-1845

* Mourning Hope Grief Center
4919 Baldwin Avenue
Lincoln, NE 68504
402-488-8989
402-486-0288 fax
http://www.mourninghope.org

Ted E. Bear Hollow
347 North 76th Street
Omaha, NE 68114
402-502-2773
402-502-4564 fax
http://www.tedebearhollow.org

Nevada
Horizon Hospice
PO Box 5361
Elko, NV 89802
775-778-0612
775-777-3648 fax

* Solacetree, Inc.
PO Box 2944
Reno, NV 89505
775-324-7723
775-324-7725 fax
http://www.solacetree.org

New Hampshire
* Pete's Place
30 St. Thomas Street, Suite 240
Dover, NH 03820
603-740-2689
603-742-7210 fax

Bridges for Children & Teens
Seacoast Hospice
10 Hampton Road
Exeter, NH 03833
603-778-7391
603-772-7692 fax
http://www.seacoasthospice.org

Hospice at HCS
69 Island Street
Keene, NH 03431
603-352-2253
800-541-4145 toll-free

Hospice of Cheshire County
7 Center Street
Keene, NH 03431
603-257-1314

VNA of Manchester and South-
  ern New Hampshire, Inc.
Stepping Stones
33 South Commercial Street,
  Suite 401
Manchester, NH 03101
603-622-3781
603-641-4074 fax

Good Grief Program
Home Health & Hospice Care
80 Continental Boulevard
Merrimack, NH 03054

603-424-3822
http://www.hhhc.org

New Jersey
The Wellness Community of
  Central New Jersey
3 Crossroads Drive
Bedminster, NJ 07921
908-658-5400, ext. 2
http://www
  .thewellnesscommunity.org

JFK Medical Center
Haven Hospice
65 James Street
Edison, NJ 08818-3059
732-321-7769
732-205-1478 fax

Sudden Unexplained Death in
  Childhood Program
30 Prospect Avenue
Hackensack, NJ 07601
800-620-SUDC (800-620-7832)
  toll-free

* The Alcove Center for Grieving Children & Families
950 Tilton Road
Northfield, NJ 08225
609-484-1133
609-484-3188 fax
http://www.thealcove.org

The Children's Art Therapy
  Program
Jane Booker Cancer Center
1 Riverview Plaza
Red Bank, NJ 07701
732-530-2382
732-224-3900 fax
http://www.meridianhealth.com

* Good Grief, Inc.
561 Springfield Avenue
Summit, NJ 07901
908-522-1999
908-522-1990 fax
http://www.good-grief.org

New Mexico
* Children's Grief Center of New
  Mexico, Inc
3020 Morris NE
Albuquerque, NM 87111
505-323-0478
505-298-6132 fax
http://childrensgrief.org

* Gerard's House
PO Box 28693
Santa Fe, NM 87592
505-424-1800
505-424-7547 fax
http://www.gerardshouse.org

New York
Pastoral Care Department
St. Mary's Hospital for Children
29-01 216th Street
Bayside, NY 11360
718-281-8852
718-279-2141 fax
http://www.stmaryskids.org

Pastoral Care Department
Bereavement Services
* Calvary Hospital
1740 Eastchester Road
Bronx, NY 10461
718-518-2000
877-4Calvary (877-422-5827)
  toll-free
718-518-2552 fax
http://www.calvaryhospital.org

Bereavement Center for Support
   & Healing
66 Boerum Place
Brooklyn, NY 11201
718-722-6214
718-722-6233 fax
http://www.ccbq.org/bereavement
   .htm

Metropolitan Jewish Hospice of
   Greater New York
6323 Seventh Avenue
Brooklyn, NY 11220-4711
718-921-7900
718-759-4181 fax
http://www.metropolitanhospice
   .org

Storm Clouds & Rainbows
Life Transitions Center
150 Bennett Road
Cheektowaga, NY 14227
716-836-6460
716-836-1578 fax
http://www.palliativecare.org

Circle of Daughters, Inc.
4637 Ironwood Drive
Hamburg, NY 14075
716-627-4934
716-648-6898 fax

The Wounded Healers' Bereavement Support Group, Inc.
511 Westlake Street
Horseheads, NY 14845
607-796-2795
http://www.woundedhealers.com

* The Sanctuary
PO Box 795
Larchmont, NY 10538-1448
914-834-4906
914-834-6763 fax
http://www.thesanctuaryforgrief
   .org

Center for Living with Loss
Hospice & Palliative Care Asso-
   ciates for CNY
990 Seventh North Street
Liverpool, NY 13088-6168
315-634-1100
315-634-1108 fax
http://www.hospicecny.org

* The Children's Grieving Center
Hospice of Orange & Sullivan
   Counties
800 Stony Brook Court
Newburgh, NY 12550
800-924-0157 toll-free
845-561-2179 fax
http://www.hospiceoforange.com

United Hospice of Rockland,
Healing Hearts Program
11 Stokum Lane
New City, NY 10956
845-634-4974, ext. 158
http://www.hospiceofrockland.org

* Center for Hope
Schneider Children's Hospital
270-06 76th Avenue
New Hyde Park, NY 11040
718-470-3123

A Caring Hand
The Billy Esposito Bereavement
Center
305 Seventh Avenue, 16th floor
New York, NY 10001
212-561-0622
http://www.acaringhand.org

American Foundation for Suicide
Prevention
120 Wall Street, 22nd Floor
New York, NY 10005
888-333-AFSP (888-333-2377)
toll-free
212-363-6237 fax

Jewish Board of Family & Children Services
Loss & Bereavement Program
120 West 57th Street, 9th floor
New York, NY 10019
212-632-4692
212-307-7896 fax
http://www.jbfcs.org

Visiting Nurse Hospice Care
Bereavement Program
1250 Broadway
New York, NY 10001-3797
212-609-1979
212-290-3933 fax
http://www.vnsny.org/mainsite/
services/s_hospice.html

* Catskill Area Hospice and Palliative Care, Inc.
542 Main Street
Oneonta, NY 13820
607-432-6773
607-431-2351 fax
http://www.cahpc.org

Hospice, Inc. Bereavement
    Department
374 Violet Avenue
Poughkeepsie, NY 12601
845-473-2273, ext. 1145
800-522-9132 toll-free
845-790-0006 fax
http://www.hospiceinc.org

Good Shepherd Hospice
4747-20 Nesconset Highway
Port Jefferson Station, NY 11776
631-474-4040
631-474-4058 fax
http://goodshepherdhospice.chsli
    .org

The Schnurmacher Family Be-
    reavement and Trauma Center
North Shore Child and Family
    Guidance Center
480 Old Westbury Road
Roslyn Heights, NY 11577
516-626-1971
516-626-8043 fax
http://www
    .northshorechildguidance.org

New Insights, Inc.
PO Box 5027
Saratoga Springs, NY 12866

518-893-2012
518-893-2558 fax

Grieving Children's Program
* Haven Grief Counseling
    Center
703 Union Street
Schenectady, NY 12305
518-370-1666
518-370-1666 fax
http://www.havengrief
    counselingcenter.org

Hope for Bereaved, Inc.
1500 Onondaga Boulevard
Syracuse, NY 13219
315-475-9675
315-475-3298 fax
http://www.hopeforbereaved.com

The Tree House Program
Bereavement Center of West-
    chester
69 Main Street
Tuckahoe, NY 10707
914-961-2818, ext. 317
914-961-8654 fax
http://www
    .thebereavementcenter.org

Hospice Care Network
900 Merchants Concourse
Westbury, NY 11590
516-832-7100
516-832-7160 fax
http://www.hospicecarenetwork.org

* The Caring Circle
45 Park Avenue
Yonkers, NY 10701
914-666-4228
914-666-0378 fax
http://www.hospiceofwestchester
   .com

North Carolina
Kids Path
CarePartners Health Services,
   Hospice and Palliative Care
68 Sweeten Creek Road
Asheville, NC 28803
828-251-0126
828-285-9798 fax
http://www.kidspath.com

* KinderMourn, Inc.
1320 Harding Plaace
Charlotte, NC 28204
704-376-2580
704-376-0149 fax
http://www.kindermourn.org

Kids Path
2504 Summit Avenue
Greensboro, NC 27405
336-544-5437
336-544-2270 fax
http://www.kidspath.com

Reflections, A Caring Program
   for Children
Hospice of Wake County
1300 Saint Mary's Street, 4th
   floor
Raleigh, NC 27605
888-900-3959 toll-free
919-828-0664 fax
http://www.hospiceofwake.org

The Sunrise Kids
Lower Cape Fear Hospice
725A Wellington Avenue
Wilmington, NC 28405
910-772-5463
800-733-7476 toll-free
910-763-5999 fax
http://www
   .hospiceandlifecarecenter.org

Carousel Center
Hospice & Palliative Care Center
101 Hospice Lane
Winston-Salem, NC 27103-3212
336-768-3972
336-659-0461 fax
http://www.hospicecarecenter.org

North Dakota
Hospice of the Red River Valley
Children's Bereavement Program
1701 38th Street SW, Suite 201
Fargo, ND 58103
800-237-4629 toll-free
701-356-1592 fax
http://www.hrrv.org

Hospice
Altru Health Systems
1380 South Columbia Road
Grand Forks, ND 58206
701-780-5258
800-545-5615 toll-free
701-780-5849 fax
http://www.altru.org

Ohio
Family Ties
Child Guidance and Family
   Solutions
682 East Buchtel Avenue
Akron, OH 44304
330-762-2557
330-535-5842 fax
http://www.cgfs.org

Hospice of North Central Ohio
1050 Dauch Drive
Ashland, OH 44805
419-281-7107
800-952-2207 toll-free
419-281-8427 fax
http://www
   .hospiceofnorthcentralohio.org

Joel's Place for Children
PO Box 180
Avon, OH 44011
440-934-1353
http://www.joelsplaceforchildren
   .com

* Fernside: A Center for Grieving
  Children
4380 Malsbary Road, Suite 300
Cincinnati, OH 45242-5644
513-745-0111
513-745-0524 fax
http://www.fernside.org

Hospice of Cincinnati
Expressions Program
4310 Cooper Road
Cincinnati, OH 45242
513-792-6914
http://www.hospiceofcincinnati
  .org

* Cornerstone of Hope
5905 Brecksville Road
Cleveland, OH 44131
216-524-3787
http://www.cornerstoneofhope.org

Hospice of the Western Reserve
19201 Villaview Road
Cleveland, OH 44119-1330
216-486-6287
216-481-4987 fax
http://www.hospicewr.org

Hospice of the Western Reserve
300 East 185 Street
Cleveland, OH 44119
800-707-8922 toll-free
216-383-3750 fax
http://www.hospicewr.org

Hospice at Riverside and Grant
Stepping Stones/Pathfinders
  Program
3595 Olentangy River Road
Columbus, OH 43214
888-389-6231 toll-free
614-566-4391 fax
http://www.ohiohealth.com

* Mount Carmel Hospice Evergreen Center
1144 Dublin Road
Columbus, OH 43215
614-234-0200
614-234-0201 fax

Hospice of Dayton
324 Wilmington Avenue
Dayton, OH 45420
800-653-4490 toll-free
937-256-9802 fax
http://www.hospicedayton.org

* Oak Tree Corner, Inc.
136 Far Hills Avenue
Dayton, OH 45409
937-285-0199
937-294-8035 fax
http://www.oaktreecorner.com

Project Hope
1510 North Main Street
Dayton, OH 45406
937-277-7828
937-276-7634 fax

* Hope Center at Grady
561 West Central Avenue
Delaware, OH 43015
800-487-1115 toll-free
740-368-5225 fax

* Your Heart to Mine
Hospice at Grady
561 West Central Avenue
Delaware, OH 43015
800-487-1115 toll-free
614-363-3175 fax

* State of the Heart Hospice
1350 North Broadway
Greenville, OH 45331
937-548-2999
937-548-7144 fax
http://www.stateoftheheartcare.org/

Hospice of the Western Reserve
5786 Heisley Road
Mentor, OH 44060
800-707-8922 toll-free
440-975-0655 fax
http://www.hospicewr.org

Good Grief Club
Stein Hospice
1200 Sycamore Lane
Sandusky, OH 44870
419-625-5269
419-625-5761 fax
http://www.steinhospice.org

Hospice of the Western Reserve
4110 Warrensville Center Road
Building A, Lobby A
Warrensville Heights, OH 44122
800-707-8922 toll-free
216-283-3181 fax
http://www.hospicewr.org

Hospice of the Western Reserve
29101 Health Campus Drive,
    Suite 400
Westlake, OH 44145-5268
440-892-6680
800-707-8922 toll-free
440-892-6690 fax
http://www.hospicewr.org

Oklahoma
The Kids' Place of Edmond
801 South Bryant
Edmond, OK 73034
405-844-5437

* Kaleidoscope
PO Box 720314
Norman, OK 73072
405-306-0052

* Calm Waters Center for
  Children and Families
4334 Northwest Expressway,
  Suite 101
Oklahoma City, OK 73116
405-841-4800
405-841-4803 fax
http://www.calmwaters.org

The Tristesse Grief Center, Inc.
1709 South Baltimore
Tulsa, OK 74119
918-587-1200
918-587-1205 fax
http://www.thetristessecenter.org

Oregon
* Hope House
Lutheran Community Services
3107 Grand Avenue
Astoria, OR 97103

503-325-6754
503-338-6268 fax

Hospice of Bend/La Pine
2075 Northeast Wyatt Court
Bend, OR 97701
541-383-3910
800-383-3910 toll-free
541-388-4221 fax
http://www.hospicebendlapine.org

* Light House Center
1620 Thompson Road
Coos Bay, OR 97420
541-269-2986
541-267-0458 fax

* Courageous Kids/Hospice of
  Sacred Heart
1121 Fairfield Avenue
Eugene, OR 97402
541-461-7577
541-461-7697 fax
http://www.peacehealth.org

Good Grief—Lovejoy Hospice
939 Southeast 8th Street
Grants Pass, OR 97526
541-474-1193
888-758-8569 toll-free
541-474-3035 fax
http://www.lovejoyhospice.org

* Winterspring
PO Box 8169
Medford, OR 97501
541-552-0620
541-245-3454 fax
http://www.winterspring.org

Early Childhood Council
2001 Southwest Nye Avenue
Pendleton, OR 97801
541-966-3133
541-276-4252 fax

St. Anthony Hospital Hospice
1601 Southeast Court Avenue
Pendleton, OR 97801
541-278-6571
541-278-3223 fax

* Dougy Center
PO Box 86852
Portland, OR 97286
503-775-5683
866-775-5683 toll-free
503-777-3097 fax
http://www.dougy.org

Me, Too. & Company
PO Box 10796
Portland, OR 97296
503-228-2104
http://www.oregonhospice.org

Mourning Resources, Inc.
PO Box 82573
Portland, OR 97202
503-777-0433

* Mercy Medical Center Hospice
Wings of Hope
2400 Stewart Parkway
Roseburg, OR 97470
541-677-2384
541-580-0175 fax

* Mother Oak's Child Center for
  Grieving Children
Willamette Valley Hospice
1015 3rd Street NW
Salem, OR 97304
503-588-3600
800-555-2431 toll-free
503-363-3891 fax
http://www.wvh.org

Pennsylvania
* Home Nursing Agency Healing
  Patch
213 Lakemont Park Boulevard
Altoona, PA 16602
814-946-5411
http://homenursingagency.com

St. Luke's VNA Hospice
1510 Valley Center Parkway,
  Suite 200
Bethlehem, PA 18017
610-954-2727

* Highmark Caring Place
Bayview Office Park, Building 2
510 Cranberry Street, Suite 200
Erie, PA 16507
866-212-4673 toll-free
http://www.highmarkcaringplace
  .com/

Precious Gems Supportive Services
231 South Easton Road, 3rd floor
Glenside, PA 19038
888-526-6958 toll-free
215-887-3820 fax
http://www.preciousgems.org

Pinnacle Health Hospice
Children & Teen Bereavement
Camps & Groups
3705 Elmwood Drive
Harrisburg, PA 17110
800-889-1098 toll-free
http://www.pinnaclehealth.org

Coping Kids Program
PATHways Center for Grief and
  Loss
Hospice of Lancaster County
685 Good Drive
Lancaster, PA 17604-4125
717-295-3900
717-391-9573 fax
http://www.hospiceoflancaster.org

* Highmark Caring Place
3 Walnut Street, Suite 200
Lemoyne, PA 17043
866-613-4673 toll-free
http://www.highmarkcaringplace
  .com/

Mommy's Light Lives On
PO Box 494
Lionville, PA 19353
610-725-9790
http://www.mommyslight.org

Sun Home Health Hospice
PO Box 232
61 Duke Street
Northumberland, PA 17857
570-286-1596
http://www.sunhomehealth.com

* Center for Grieving Children,
   Teens & Families
1139 East Luzerne Street
Philadelphia, PA 19124
215-744-4025
215-744-4027 fax
http://www.grievingchildren.org

* Children's Hospital of Philadelphia
Bereavement Program
34th & Civic Center Boulevard
Philadelphia, PA 19104-4399
215-590-3273
215-590-2066 fax
http://www.chop.edu

* Highmark Caring Place
620 Stanwix Street
Pittsburg, PA 15222

888-224-4673 toll-free
http://www.highmarkcaringplace
   .com

* Peter's Place
Center for Grieving Children &
   Families
150 North Radnor-Chester Road,
   Suite F130
Radnor, PA 19087
610-687-5150
610-687-5120 fax
http://www.petersplaceonline.org

Center for Loss and Bereavement
3847 Skippack Pike
Skippack, PA 19474
610-222-4110
http://www.bereavementcenter
   .org

Tides-: A Support Program for
   Grieving Children and the
   People Who Love Them
PO Box 1251
State College, PA 16804
814-692-2233
866-883-8608 toll-free
www.tidesprogram.org

* Daddy's Spirit Moves Me Forward
PO Box 80022
Valley Forge, PA 19484
610-710-1477
610-827-7437 fax
http://www.daddysspirit.org

* Hospice Care, Inc.
10 Leet Street
Washington, PA 15301
724-250-4500
http://www.welnet.org

* Safe Harbor Program
Abington Memorial Health
Center
Willow Wood Building, Suite 225
2510 Maryland Road
Willow Grove, PA 19090
215-481-5983
215-481-5910 fax
http://www.amh.org/

Olivia's House
830 South George Street
York, PA 17403
717-699-1133
http://www.oliviashouse.org

Rhode Island
Friends Way
765 West Shore Road
Warwick, RI 02889
401-921-0980
http://www.friendsway.org

South Carolina
Jaime's Tree House (Bereavement
Camp)
Hospice of Laurens County
1304 Springdale Drive
Clinton, SC 29325
864-833-6287
http://www
.hospiceoflaurenscounty.com

Good Grieving: Helping Children and Teens
South Carolina Cancer Center
7 Richland Medical Park Drive
Columbia, SC 29203
803-434-3500
803-434-7291 fax
http://www.sccancercenter.org

Hospice & Community Care
PO Box 993
Rock Hill, SC 29731
803-329-4663
800-895-2273 toll-free
http://www
   .hospicecommunitycare.org

Friends of Caroline Hospice
Child Bereavement Program
1110-13 Street
Port Royal, SC 29935
843-525-6257
http://carolinehospice.org

Tennessee
Compassion Connection, Inc.:
   A Center for Loss
271 Medical Park Boulevard
Bristol, TN 37620
423-383-1322
423-274-0532 fax

The Grief Center
Alive Hospice, Inc.
1718 Patterson
Nashville, TN 37203
615-327-1085
800-327-1085 toll-free
615-321-8902 fax
http://www.alivehospice.org

Texas
The Hope & Healing Place
1721 South Tyler
Amarillo, TX 79102
806-371-8998
806-371-8948 fax
http://www.hopeandhealingplace
   .org

Hospice Austin
4107 Spicewood Springs Road,
   Suite 100
Austin, TX 78759
512-342-4700
512-795-9055 fax
http://www.hospiceaustin.org

My Healing Place
16042 Fontaine Avenue
Austin, TX 78734
512-347-7878
http://www.myhealingplace.org

Elijah's Place
2780 Eastex Freeway
Beaumont, TX 77703
409-924-4419

Camp Sol
2904 Floyd Street, Suite D3
Dallas, TX 75204
214-442-1664
http://www.campsol.org

* Dallas Kids GriefWorks
Christian Services
6320 LBJ Freeway, Suite 122
Dallas, TX 75240
972-960-9981
800-375-2229 toll-free
972-960-0062 fax
http://www.christianservices-sw
   .org

Camp El Tesoro de la Vida
Camp Fire USA First Texas
   Council
2700 Meacham Boulevard
Fort Worth, TX 76137-4699
817-831-2111, ext. 158
817-831-5070 fax
http://www.campeltesoro.org

* The Warm Place
809 Lipscomb Street
Fort Worth, TX 76104-2710
817-870-2272
817-870-2570 fax
http://www.thewarmplace.org

* Bo's Place
10050 Buffalo Speedway
Houston, TX 77054
713-942-8339
713-942-2252 fax
http://www.bosplace.org

* Gili's Place for the Bereaved
PO Box 20712
Houston, TX 77225
713-661-9209
713-669-0567 fax
http://www.gilisplace.com

Wings Program
Houston Hospice
1905 Holcombe Boulevard
Houston, TX 77030
713-677-7131
http://www.houstonhospice.org

Hope Hospice Children's Grief
   Program
611 North Walnut Avenue
New Braunfels, TX 78130
830-625-7525
800-499-7501 toll-free
830-606-1388 fax
http://www.hopehospice.net

Project Joy and Hope for Texas
PO Box 5111
Pasadena, TX 77508
713-944-6JOY (713-944-6569)
866-JOY HOPE (866-569-4673)
 toll-free
http://www.joyandhope.org

Journey of Hope Grief Support
 Center, Inc.
3900 West 15th Street, Suite 306
Plano, TX 75075
972-964-1600
972-964-1602 fax
http://www.johgriefsupport.org

Building Bridges
Hospice of San Angelo
PO Box 471
San Angelo, TX 76902
325-658-6524
325-659-2023 fax

The Children's Bereavement
 Center of South Texas
332 West Craig Place
San Antonio, TX 78212
210-736-HUGS (210-736-4847)
210-738-9019 fax
http://www.cbcst.org

* The Cooper Foundation
PO Box 953
Tomball, TX 77377
832-623-9966
281-873-5544 fax
http://www.thecooperfoundation
 .org/

Wings Children's Grief Program
Hospice of East Texas
4111 University Boulevard
Tyler, TX 75701
903-266-3400
903-566-5853 fax
http://www.hospiceofeasttexas.org

Utah
Canary Garden
PO Box 53
Lehi, UT 84043
801-361-8758
http://www.canarygarden.org

Grief Center
1050 East South Temple
Salt Lake City, UT 84102
801-350-4191

Primary Children's Medical
   Center
100 Medical Drive
Salt Lake City, UT 84113
801-588-3483
801-588-3629 fax

* The Sharing Place
1695 East 3300 South
Salt Lake City, UT 84106
801-466-6730
801-466-0422 fax
http://www.thesharingplace.org

* Family Summit Foundation
A Center for Grieving Children
560 39th Street
South Ogden, UT 84403
801-476-1127
801-476-1149 fax
http://www.familysummit.com

Virginia
* Kids' Haven: A Center for
   Grieving Children
325 12th Street
Lynchburg, VA 24504
434-845-4072
434-845-8733 fax
www.kidshavenlynchburg.org

Kidz 'N Grief
Bon Secours Hospice
2 Bernardine Drive
Newport News, VA 23602
757-886-6613
757-886-6615 fax

The Comfort Zone Camp
2101-A Westmoreland Street
Richmond, VA 23230
804-377-3430
866-488-5679 toll-free
804-377-3433 fax
http://www.comfortzonecamp.org

Good Samaritan Hospice
Bereavement Services
3825 Electric Road, Suite A
Roanoke, VA 24018
540-776-0198
540-776-0841 fax
http://www.goodsamaritanhospice
   .org

Fairfax County Mental Health
Community Services Board
8348 Traford Lane, Suite 400
Springfield, VA 22152
703-866-2119
703-451-7539 fax

* Jewish Family Service of Tide-
water, Inc.
260 Grayson Road
Virginia Beach, VA 23462
757-459-4640
757-459-4643 fax
http://www.jfshamptonroads.org

Vermont
Cove/Champlain Valley
PO Box 136
Huntington, VT 05462
802-434-4159

* Center for Creative Healing
114 Westminster Road
Putney, VT 05346
802-387-2550

Washington
* GriefWorks: A Bereavement
Resource
PO Box 912
Auburn, WA 98071-0912
253-333-9420
800-850-9420 toll-free (WA only)
http://www.griefworks.org

Lisa's Kids
PMB 566
1225 East Sunset Drive, Suite 145
Bellingham, WA 98226

360-715-2597
360-738-9128 fax

Providence Hospice of
Snohomish County
2731 Wetmore Avenue, Suite 520
Everett, WA 98201-3581
425-261-4777
425-261-4869 fax
http://www.providence.org

* The Chaplaincy
Cork's Place
2108 West Entiat
Kennewick, WA 99336
509-783-7416
509-735-7850 fax
http://www.tricitieschaplaincy.org

* Community Home Health and
Hospice
1035 11th Avenue
PO Box 2067
Longview, WA 98632
360-425-8510
360-414-5434 fax
http://www.chhh.org

* Center for Counseling and
  Development
Safe Harbor
1021 Legion Way SE
Olympia, WA 98501-1522
360-754-0820
360-352-7319 fax

Sound Care Kids
PO Box 5008
Olympia, WA 98509
360-493-5928
360-493-5924 fax
http://www.providence.org

* Annie Tran Centers for Grief
  & Loss
2001 Paterson Road
Prosser, WA 99350
509-786-7100
509-786-7959 fax

* Healing Center
6409 1/2 Roosevelt Way NE
Seattle, WA 98115
206-523-1206
206-523-1808 fax
http://www.healingcenterseattle
  .org

* Journey Program
Children's Hospital Regional
  Medical Center
4800 Sandpoint Way NE
Seattle, WA 98105-9907
206-987-2062
866-987-2000 toll-free
206-987-2246 fax
http://www.seattlechildrens.org

Providence Hospice of Seattle
Safe Crossings
425 Pontius Avenue N, Suite 200
Seattle, WA 98109
206-320-4000
206-320-7333 fax

Rise n' Shine
417 23rd Avenue S
Seattle, WA 98144
206-628-8949
206-628-6207 fax
http://www.risenshine.org

* WICS
PO Box 66896
Seattle, WA 98166
206-241-5650
http://www.kcwics.org

* The Landing: A Healing Place
  for Kids
2000 Hospital Drive
Sedro Woolley, WA 98284
360-420-9390
http://www
  .unitedgeneralhospitalfounda
  tion.org

Kid's Grief Group
Hospice of Kitsap County
3100 Bucklin Hill Road, Suite
  201
Silverdale, WA 98383
360-698-4611
360-692-1893 fax
http://www.hospiceofkitsapcounty
  .org

* BRIDGES: A Center for Grieving Children
310 North K Street
Tacoma, WA 98403
253-403-1837
253-272-8266 toll-free
253-305-0868 fax
http://www.multicase.org

* Stepping Stones
Southwest Washington Medical
  Center
PO Box 1600
Vancouver, WA 98663

360-696-5120
360-696-5038 fax

Camp Amanda
Walla Walla Community Hospice
PO Box 2026
Walla Walla, WA 99362
509-525-5561
509-525-3517 fax
http://www.wwhospice.org

Griefbusters
Walla Walla Community Hospice
PO Box 2026
Walla Walla, WA 99362
509-525-5561
509-525-3717 fax
http://www.wwhospice.org

* The Good Grief Center
1610 5th Street
Wenatchee, WA 98801
509-662-6069
503-662-8339 fax
http://www.goodgriefcenter.org

Wisconsin
Center for Grieving Children
117 South Locust Street
Appleton, WI 54914
920-731-0555
920-968-2716 fax
http://www.bgclubfoxvalley.org/
    main.asp?id=21

Faith's Lodge
6942 County Road C
Danbury, WI 54830
715-866-8200
715-866-8250 fax
http://www.faithslodge.org

Unity Hospice and Palliative
    Care
2366 Oak Ridge Circle
De Pere, WI 54115
800-990-9249 toll-free
920-338-8111 fax
http://www.unityhospice.org

Margaret Ann's Place
912 North Hawley Road
Milwaukee, WI 53213
414-732-2663
866-455-HOPE (866-455-4673)
    toll-free
http://www.margaretannsplace.org

Care Connection—Community
    Memorial Hospital
W180 N8085 Town Hall Road
Menomonee Falls, WI 53052-
    0408
262-251-1001
262-250-7448 fax
http://www.communitymemorial
    .com

Children's Hospital of Wisconsin
Bereavement Services
Family Services Department
9000 West Wisconsin Avenue
Milwaukee, WI 53201
414-266-2995
414-266-3338 fax
http://www.chw.org

* My Good Mourning Place
4005 West Oklahoma Avenue
Milwaukee, WI 53215
414-643-5678

St. Luke's Hospital
2900 West Oklahoma Avenue
Milwaukee, WI 53215
414-649-6634
414-649-5420 fax

Camp Hope
301 Florence Drive
Stevens Point, WI 54481
715-341-0076
http://www.camphopeforkids.org

* Kyle's Korner
7016 West North Avenue
Wauwatosa, WI 53213
414-777-1585
http://www.kyleskorner.com

∞ RESOURCES ∞

BOOKS TO CONSIDER READING ALONG THE JOURNEY

The books listed here offer solace, reassurance, and helpful information for your journey. They are divided into three categories: For Children and Teens, For Parenting Your Grieving Child, and For You as You Grieve. While some of these books may be available at your local bookstore or library, most can be ordered online from either Compassion Books (www.compassion books.com) or The Centering Corporation (www.centeringcorp .com).

FOR CHILDREN AND TEENS

The following books can help you have a meaningful conversation with your child about the facts of death and the feelings associated with grief. I've indicated which are read-aloud books and which are for older children. Before sharing any book with your child, read it first to make sure you agree with its message.

Tell Me, Papa
By Joy and Marv Johnson

Publisher: Center for Thanatology Research & Education, Revised edition (2001)

For young children through primary school age, this read-along book provides basic, concrete information about the meaning of death and what to expect at wakes, funerals, and burials. It also gives basic information about cremations. This book will also help your child make his or her own decision about whether or not to attend a death ritual.

Where's Jess?
By Joy and Marv Johnson
Publisher: Centering Corporation; Revised edition (1982)

This read-along book is for two- to five-year-olds whose sibling has died. It will help you explain what has happened in your family and normalize painful feelings that accompany loss.

Waterbugs and Dragonflies: Explaining Death to Young Children
By Doris Stickney
Publisher: Pilgrim Press (1997)

For young children, this short, classic, read-along book uses waterbugs and dragonflies to explain death and spiritual transformation from a Christian perspective.

When Dinosaurs Die: A Guide to Understanding Death
By Laurie Krasny Brown and Marc Brown
Publisher: Little, Brown Young Readers (1998)

This is one of my favorite illustrated books about death and dying. Despite the seriousness of the subject matter, it manages to stay lighthearted. It is likely to intrigue readers of all ages, from young children to adults, and covers a broad range of religious beliefs, cultural practices, and reasons why people die ranging from illness, accident, substance abuse, suicide, and murder.

Lifetimes: The Beautiful Way to Explain Death to Children
By Bryan Mellonie and Robert Ingpen
Publisher: Bantam Books (1983)

This is an illustrated book for six- to nine-year-olds that takes a scientific approach to death education, explaining that every life form, including humans, has "a beginning and an end and living in between." If the knowledge that everyone must die someday has been worrying your child, then this book will help put things in perspective.

Aarvy Aardvark Finds Hope
By Donna O'Toole
Kore Loy McWhirter, illustrator
Publisher: Compassion Books (1988)

This illustrated storybook is appropriate for children of all ages. It touches the heart while teaching about the grieving process and the meaning of true friendship. Read this one aloud to your child.

Children Also Grieve: Talking about Death and Healing
By Linda Goldman
Publisher: Jessica Kingsley Publishers (2005)

This interactive storybook helps young children come to terms with a significant death in their lives. One section is designed as a memory book with excellent prompts that will inspire reflection and reminiscence. There is also a section to help adults support their grieving children.

What Is Death?
By Etan Boritzer
Nancy Forrest, illustrator
Publisher: Veronica Lane Books (2000)

This whimsically illustrated little book is appropriate for all age groups. It is an existential/spiritual meditation on the meaning of death that includes commentary on Hindu, Buddhist, Christian, Jewish, Islamic, and atheistic traditions.

Our Special Garden: Understanding Cremation
By Karen L. Carney
Publisher: Dragonfly Publishing (1997)

This is the best book I've found for explaining cremation to young children and is written with remarkable attention to age-appropriate language. Please note that the author makes reference to the soul and heaven to explain the meaning of death.

What Is Cancer, Anyway?: Explaining Cancer to Children of All Ages
By Karen Carney
Publisher: Dragonfly Publishing (1998)

This coloring book for young children covers technical information about cancer in a frank and comforting manner. If a loved one is facing cancer, this will be informative and reassuring to your child.

What Does That Mean?
By Joy Johnson and Howard Ivan Smith
Publisher: Centering Corporation (2007)

If your child has been asking difficult questions about death and dying, then this book will help you explain a whole range of death-related terms.

Saying Goodbye
By Jim and Joan Boulden
Publisher: Boulden Publishing; Revised edition (1992)

Written for five- to eight-year-olds, this book helps explain that death is final.

Goodbye Forever
By Jim and Joan Boulden

Publisher: Boulden Publishing (1994)

Written for five- to eight-year-olds, this book helps explain the concept of death and how to say good-bye to a loved one who is dying.

I Heard Your Daddy Died
By Mark Scrivani
Publisher: Centering Corporation (1996)

For two- to six-year-olds when a father dies.

I Heard Your Mommy Died
By Mark Scrivani
Publisher: Centering Corporation (1994)

For two- to six-year-olds when a mother dies.

No New Baby: For Siblings Who Have a Brother or Sister Die Before Birth
By Marilyn Gryte
Publisher: Centering Corporation (1988)

For two- to six-year-olds when a sibling dies due to a miscarriage.

The Saddest Time
By Norma Simon
Publisher: Albert Whitman & Company (1992)

Written for older children and preteens, it includes three short stories that sensitively deal with the death of an uncle with a terminal illness, a classmate killed in an accident, and an elderly grandparent.

Finding Grandpa Everywhere: A Young Child Discovers Memories of a Grandparent
By John Hodge
Publisher: Centering Corporation (1998)

Written for children of primary school age, this storybook will help you explain the importance of keeping memories alive.

Learning to Say Good-by: When a Parent Dies
By Eda LeShan
Publisher: Demco Media (1988)

Written for children eight years old through teens, it offers caring support and advice after a parent dies. Of all the books I read shortly after my own father's death, this was most helpful to me, even though I was a young adult at the time.

A Complete Book About Death for Kids
By Earl Grollman, Joy Johnson, and Brad Donner
Publisher: Centering Corporation (2006)

This practical guide for grieving children was written by experts in the field of childhood bereavement.

Am I Still a Sister?
By Alicia Sims
Publisher: Big A and Company (1988)

A very wise eleven-year-old wrote this book after her brother died. It is an extraordinary meditation on the meaning of death, appropriate for six-year-olds through adults.

My Grandson Lew
By Charlotte Zolotow
Publisher: HarperCollins Children's Books; Revised edition (2007)

This is a beautifully written picture book about a six-year-old boy's memories of his grandfather who died four years earlier. Read this with a child of any age.

Saying Good-bye to Grandma
By Jane Resh Thomas
Mary Sewall, illustrator
Publisher: Sandpiper (1990)

This small chapter book, for children of all ages, tells of a young girl recalling her grandmother's funeral. It demonstrates how childhood play is often an integral part of a young person's way of grieving.

To Hell with Dying
By Alice Walker
Catherine Deeter, illustrator
Publisher: Voyager Books (1993)

For children, teens, and adults, this is the story of a young African-American woman and her eccentric elderly neighbor. Alice Walker has written a deeply moving narrative about unconditional love. The illustrations are gorgeous.

Losing Uncle Tim
By Mary Kate Jordan
Judith Friedman, illustrator
Publisher: Albert Whitman & Company (1993)

For primary school children through teens, this is the story of a boy who learns that his favorite uncle is dying of AIDS.

Be a Friend: Children Who Live with HIV Speak
Edited by Lori S. Wiener, Aprille Best, Philip A. Pizzo
Publisher: Albert Whitman & Company (1996)

Includes poetry and narratives from young people whose lives are impacted by HIV-AIDS. For older children and teens.

But I Didn't Say Goodbye: For Parents and Professionals Helping Child Suicide Survivors
By Barbara Rubel
Publisher: Griefwork Center Inc. (2000)

For older children and young teens, this is the story of a ten-year-old boy whose father died from suicide. Each section of this book ends with activities and conversation starters. Read this with your child if suicide has touched your lives.

Grandpa Loved
By Josephine Nobisso
Maureen Hyde, illustrator
Publisher: Gingerbread House (2000)

For children of all ages, this uplifting picture book about memory keeping celebrates the loving relationship of a young boy and his grandfather.

Facing Change: Falling Apart and Coming Together Again in the Teen Years
By Donna O'Toole
Publisher: Compassion Books (1995)

This excellent little handbook addresses a whole range of losses and is small enough for your teen to slip into a back pocket. Packed with lots of wisdom and food for thought.

How It Feels When a Parent Dies
By Jill Krementz
Publisher: Knopf (1988)

For older children and teens, this is a series of first-person narratives written by young people ranging in age from nine to sixteen, all who've had a parent die. Photographs and names of each young contributor will convince any skeptical reader that these are true stories.

Beyond the Rainbow: A Workbook for Children in the Advanced Stages of a Very Serious Illness
By Marge Eaton Heegaard
Publisher: Fairview Press (2003)

This is a workbook for older children and young teens who have already been informed of their life-threatening illness. It provides writing prompts to help a child explore thoughts and feelings.

Remember the Secret
By Elisabeth Kübler-Ross
Heather Preston, illustrator
Publisher: Celestial Arts (1998)

For children of all ages, this is an uplifting story of love and faith. In it, two young friends discover that one of them is dying.

When Something Terrible Happens
By Marge Heegard
Publisher: Woodland Press (1992)

This is an activity book for young children learning to face something tragic in their lives.

After a Suicide: A Workbook for Grieving Children
After a Murder: A Workbook for Grieving Children
By The Dougy Center
Publisher: The Dougy Center (2001)

For children of all ages, both of these Dougy Center workbooks address feelings and concerns of children after someone they love died from suicide or homicide. They are beautifully designed and filled with quotes from children ranging from ages five to twelve. These are excellent materials to share with your child if you face a homicide or suicide.

Healing Your Grieving Heart for Teens: One Hundred Practical Ideas
By Alan Wolfelt
Publisher: Companion Press (2007)

This is a hands-on book for your grieving teenager, packed with tips for understanding and expressing grief.

Teenagers Book About Suicide
By Earl Grollman and Joy Johnson
Publisher: Centering Corporation (2001)
    This workbook is for teens facing suicide.

You Are Not Alone
By Lynne Hughes
Publisher: Scholastic Press (2005)
    Written by the founder of Comfort Zone Camp—teens tell what it's like when a parent dies.

Helping Teens Cope with Death
By The Dougy Center
Publisher: The Dougy Center (1999)
    This collection of poetry and words of wisdom from adolescents themselves will offer your teen very helpful strategies for managing grief.

A Teen's Guide to Coping: When a Loved One Is Sick and Preparing to Die
By Fairview Hospice
Publisher: Fairview Health Services (2003)
    This hands-on booklet for teens includes a Guided Journal Section.

FOR PARENTING YOUR GRIEVING CHILD

    The following books are excellent resources for deepening your understanding of childhood and adolescent grief.

Breaking the Silence: A Guide to Helping Children with Complicated Grief—Suicide, Homicide, AIDS, Violence and Abuse
By Linda Goldman
Publisher: Brunner-Routledge; 2nd edition (2001)

Goldman, a wise and experienced clinician, has written a practical guide to help adults help children with a range of extraordinary bereavement challenges.

Children Mourning, Mourning Children
Edited by Ken Doka
Publisher: Taylor & Francis (1995)

The chapter by Ida Martinson, called "The Empty Space Phenomenon," explores getting over it, filling the emptiness, and keeping the connection.

Never Too Young to Know
By Phyllis Silverman
Publisher: Taylor & Francis (1995)

Psychologist/researcher/teacher Phyllis Silverman, a wise and sensitive observer of young people and their families, shares her research findings on childhood grief.

Helping Children Grieve and Grow
By Donna O'Toole
Publisher: Compassion Press (2007)

A practical booklet for parents of grieving children.

Helping Teens Cope with Death
By The Dougy Center
Publisher: The Dougy Center (1999)

This information-packed Dougy Center handbook will help you to understand and support your grieving teenager.

Helping Adults with Mental Retardation Grieve a Death Loss
By Charlene Luchterhand and Nancy Murphy
Publisher: Taylor & Francis (1998)

This practical handbook will help you reach out to a member of your family who is developmentally disabled.

FOR YOU AS YOU GRIEVE

The following books are divided into six categories: General Information, When Your Parent Dies, For Widows and Widowers, After a Suicide or Homicide, For Bereaved Parents, and Books to Help Clarify Meaning and Purpose.

General Information

Healing and Growing Through Grief
By Donna O'Toole
Publisher: Compassion Press (2008)

This is a practical booklet to guide you through your grief journey.

Living When a Loved One Has Died
By Earl Grollman
Publisher: Beacon Press (1997)

This is a classic from Rabbi Earl Grollman, whose gentle, honest words offer solace and hope.

How to Go On Living When Someone You Love Dies
By Therese Rando
Publisher: Bantam (1991)

Written by a very knowledgeable teacher, this invaluable guide inspires hope.

When Bad Things Happen to Good People
By Harold S. Kushner
Publisher: Anchor (2004)

Rabbi Kushner's classic book explores many of the great theological questions that often come with profound losses.

Men Don't Cry, Women Do: Transcending Gender Stereotypes of Grief
By Ken Doka and Terry Martin
Publisher: Routledge (1999)
Grief styles aren't simply determined by gender. Doka and Martin explain action-oriented grief and feeling-focused grief.

Swallowed by a Snake: The Gift of the Masculine Side of Healing
By Tom Golden
Publisher: Golden Healing Publishing (1996, 2000)
Dealing with loss through action—the masculine grief. It also addresses grief from a cross-cultural perspective.

When a Man Faces Grief: Twelve Practical Ideas to Help You Heal From Loss
By Jim Miller
Publisher: Willowgreen Publishing (1998)
This is a practical booklet for men who grieve.

When Your Parent Dies
Never the Same: Coming to Terms with the Death of a Parent
By Donna Schuurman
Publisher: St. Martin's (2003)
Written by the director of The Dougy Center, this is a hands-on book for adults who lost a parent as a child. It addresses long-term affects of childhood grief.

She Loved Me, She Loved Me Not: Adult Parent Loss After a Conflicted Relationship

By Linda Converse
Publisher: 1st Books Library (2001)

This book offers honest reflections, insight, and advice on a subject too often neglected.

For Widows and Widowers

Death Without Denial/Grief Without Apology: A Guide for Facing Grief and Loss
By Barbara K. Roberts
Publisher: NewSage Press (2002)

This touching and often humorous memoir, written by the widow of the former governor of Oregon, is filled with practical advice.

Letters to Kate: Life After Life
By Carl H. Klaus
Publisher: University of Iowa Press (2006)

This poignant memoir consists of beautifully written letters to Klaus's wife during the first year after her death.

A Handbook for Widowers
By Ed Ames
Publisher: The Centering Corporation (2004)

Ames offers a male perspective on the death of a spouse.

Widow to Widow: Thoughtful Practical Ideas for Changing Your Life
By Genevieve Davis Ginsburg
Publisher: Da Capo Press (1997)

This book offers wise and practical advice for coping with the death of a husband.

The Loss of a Life Partner: Narratives of the Bereaved
By Carolyn Ambler Walter

Publisher: Columbia University Press (2003)

Well researched and rich with narrative material, this book consists of interviews with same-sex partners as well as opposite-sex partners.

After a Suicide or Homicide

After Suicide Loss: Coping with Your Grief
By Bob Baugher and Jack Jordan

Available from Bob Baugher, Ph.D., 7108 127th Place SE, Newcastle, WA 98056-1325 or b_kbaugher@yahoo.com (2002)

This little handbook is packed with invaluable advice for the first days and months following the suicide of a loved one. Highly recommended.

Suicide of a Child: For Parents Whose Child Died by Suicide
By Adina Wrobleski
Publisher: Centering Corporation (1993)

Highly recommended for bereaved parents after a suicide.

Retelling Violent Death
By Edward Rynearson
Publisher: Routledge (2001)

This beautifully written book explains why violent deaths sometimes pose extraordinary challenges to the bereaved and suggests ways to learn to live well again. The author is a psychiatrist with a profound depth of understanding regarding traumatic grief.

No Time For Goodbyes: Coping with Sorrow, Anger, and Injustice After a Tragic Death
By Janice Harris Lord
Publisher: Compassion Press; 6th edition (2006)

This book is an essential read for families dealing with a violent death.

For Bereaved Parents

For Better or Worse: A Handbook for Couples Whose Child Has Died
By Maribeth Wilder Doerr
Publisher: Centering Corporation (1992)

Written by a bereaved mother, it addresses many challenges faced by bereaved parents, including marital stress.

A Broken Heart Still Beats: After Your Child Dies
Edited by Anne McCracken and Mary Semel
Publisher: Hazelden (2000)

This collection of essays and stories of healing and renewal are by renowned writers who have all experienced the death of a child. Contributors include Isabel Allende, Sophocles, and W.E.B. DuBois.

Dear Parents: Letters to Bereaved Parents
Edited by Joy Johnson
Publisher: Centering Corporation; Revised edition (1989)

A book of supportive letters to bereaved parents written by fifty-two bereaved parents.

Empty Arms: Coping After Miscarriage, Stillbirth and Infant Death
By Sherokee Ilse
Publisher: Wintergreen Press, Inc.; 20th Revised & enlarged edition (2000)

This is a classic, offering invaluable support to families following a pregnancy-related or infant death.

Healing a Father's Grief
By William Schatz
Publisher: Medic Publishing (1984)

This little book for bereaved fathers is loaded with practical advice from a bereaved father.

Never Too Old for a Lullaby: Death of an Adult Child
By Juanita White
Publisher: Centering Corporation (1998)

This important book underscores that parents grieve for their adult children, too.

Books That Help Clarify Meaning and Purpose After a Death

Lessons of Loss: A Guide to Coping
By Robert Neimeyer
Publisher: Center for the Study of Loss and Transition (2006)

Neimeyer is a wise teacher/researcher/psychologist who has written a beautiful guide for establishing a new sense of meaning and purpose in your life after a shattering death.

Spinning Gold Out of Straw: How Stories Heal
By Diane Rooks
Publisher: Salt Run Press (2001)

Diane Rooks teaches the reader how to create personal healing stories.

Towers of Hope: Stories to Help Us Heal
By Joy Carol
Publisher: Forest of Peace Publishing (2002)

The author recounts stories about people who suffered from tremendously difficult circumstances, and found wholeness again.

The Next Place
By Warren Hanson
Publisher: Waldman House Press (1997)

A gorgeously illustrated meditation on the journey "of light and hope where earthly hurts are left behind."

Hello From Heaven!
By Bill and Judy Guggenheim
Publisher: Bantam Books (1996)

This book documents after-death communications (ADCs), including over 350 poignant and comforting ADC accounts from contributors.

Many Lives, Many Masters: The True Story of a Prominent Psychiatrist, His Young Patient, and the Past-Life Therapy That Changed Both Their Lives
By Brian Weiss
Publisher: Fireside (1988)

This is a thought-provoking and moving account of one man's unexpected spiritual awakening.

Healing the Hurt Spirit: Daily Aspirations for People Who Have Lost a Loved One Through Suicide
By Catherine Greenleaf
Publisher: St. Dymphna Press (2006)

This book instills hope that it is possible to live a full and happy life despite suicide loss.

Spiritual Healing
By Douglas C. Smith and Theodore J. Chapin
Publisher: Psycho-Spiritual Publications (2000)

This handbook offers activities, guided imagery, meditations, and prayers for enhancing spirituality.

Embracing Life Again: Finding God Faithful in the Midst of Loss
By Gwen Bagne
Publisher: Winepress Publishing (1999)

This first-person narrative explores faith in the midst of crisis, from a Christian perspective.

Who Dies?: An Investigation of Conscious Living and Conscious Dying
By Stephen Levine
Publisher: Anchor Books (1982)

This is a beautifully written exploration of how to participate fully in life in order to prepare for whatever may come next. A Buddhist perspective on bereavement.

Family Tales, Family Wisdom: How to Gather the Stories of a Lifetime and Share Them with Your Family
By Dr. Robert U. Akeret with Daniel Klein
Publisher: William Morrow and Company, Inc. (1991)

This is a fun, practical guide to family storytelling.

The Undertaking: Life Studies From the Dismal Trade
By Thomas Lynch
Publisher: W.W. Norton & Company (1997)

Thomas Lynch, a poet/undertaker, offers wisdom and humor and hope.

. . . I Never Saw Another Butterfly: Children's Drawings and Poems from Terezin Concentration Camp, 1942–1944 Expanded 2nd Edition
Publisher: Schocken Books (1993)

This collection of children's poems and artwork from Terezin Concentration Camp is profoundly inspiring.

∞ INDEX ∞